Rachel I have [illegible] her
quite a number [illegible]
when she was a [illegible]
the Bioscience Dept of Strathclyde
University (now retired and
happily married to Prof Wallace
now retired Prof. of Mathematics
also at Strathclyde University
Rachel has a brilliant brain
Can converse in any subject
you bring up. but however
serious has the jolly knack
of finishing off with one of her
numerous jokes
I love her.
Annie Good

Sister Annie

Anne Good

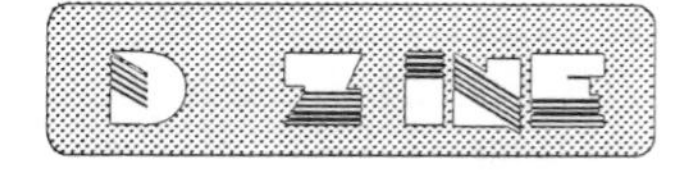

ISBN 0-9543771-0-9

Published by

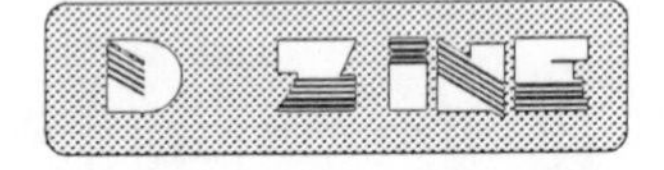

Design & Print
by
D-Zine
268 Bath Street, GLASGOW. G2 4JR
Tel/Fax: 0141 332 8507
e-mail: garyj13@hotmail.com

DEDICATION

This book is dedicated
to
my dear friend
AMELIA NATHAN HILL
1919 - 2001
Founder of
Action Against Allergies

ACKNOWLEDGEMENTS

Thanks to Dr. Ian Menzies who urged me to write this book and everyone who has helped me, especially :

Doctor Rohan Chauhan

Comunn Na Gaidhlig

The Kenyan High Commission

Beathag Mhoireasdan

Siùshadh NicCuarta

Gary Johnstone

John Nicolson

Joan MacKinnon

Donald John Smith

Anne Good, Glasgow 2002

PREFACE

It is an honour to write the foreward to this autobiography of a lady who is a legend – a legend above all in the West End of Glasgow where she now lives.

Anne Good, née Nicolson, was born in Stornoway, Isle of Lewis, in 1919. A native Gaelic speaker, she has a wealth of Gaelic heritage and culture. She is also a cosmopolitan, widely-travelled woman. She lived in Africa for several years as matron of a hospital in Kenya and ruled it with a kind but firm hand. "Strict but fair" was her nurses' verdict on her. She also made frequent visits to India, a country she knows well and loves.

She keeps open house. The place is like a fairground with the comings and goings of guests, wayfarers, waifs and strays from all over the world. Her sister, Seonaig, a staunch support and helpmeet, says "she has a heart of gold". The flat at 59 Barrington Drive has become a Mecca for the weary, the wanderer, the troubled, to say nothing of Maryhill Liberal Party which holds its regular meetings there! Anne Good's hospitality – the lavish meals, the meringues! – is boundless.

Her small, indomitable figure clad in dainty little dresses with lace collars and highlighted with a head of flaming red hair, is a familiar sight in the West End. She is a devout, church-going Christian. She has close friends of every religion.

She is a superb organiser. Jimmy Saville has nothing on Anne Good when it comes to fixing it. She rules her veritable little empire in the West End. You want a taxi, she'll get you a special taxi; you want a lodger, she'll find you the perfect lodger; you want an election agent, she'll get you the perfect election agent. She has done all these and more for me.

This book is not only the portrait of a complex and dynamic small woman. It is also a valuable record of life in Lewis in pre-war days, a life-style gone for good. Anne's powerful personality illumines it and sparkles throughout her book.

Elspeth Buchanan 2002

Roi-ràdh

'Se urram a th'ann roi-ràdh a sgrìobhadh a thaobh féin-eachdraidh thèa tha cho ainmeil ri ùghdar an leabhair seo, agus a tha gu h-àraid ainmeil ann an taobh siar Ghlaschu far a bheil i a-nis a' còmhnaidh.

Rugadh Anna NicNeacail, (a' Bh. Ph. Good) o chionn ceithir fichead bliadhna 's a h-aon ann an Steòrnabhagh an Eilean Leòdhais. Fileanta ann an Gàidhlig bho dùthchas tha i saoibhir ann an dualchas agus cultar nan Gàidheal. A thuilleadh air an sin tha eòlas aice air iomadh cultar eile bho dheifir ceàrnaidh den t-saoghal.

Chuir i seachad mòran bhliadhnaichean na banaltram ann an Afraca, na ceannard air ospadal ann an Kenya far an robh i a' riaghladh le coibhneas agus ceartas agus 'se sin an teisteanas a thug an luchd-obrach oirre. Bidh i a' siubhal gu minig dha na h-Innsean, dùthaich air a bheil i mion-eòlach agus a tha glè dhlúth dha cridhe. Bidh i a' cumail suas ri a dalta a thug i dhan t-saoghal o chionn dà fhichead bliadhna anns an ospadal ann an Kenya, agus a tha a-nis a' fuireach ann an ceann a tuath nan Innsean.

Tha an dachaigh aig Anna fosgailte dha na h-uile neach a thogras a dhol air chèilidh. Tha an taigh aice daonnan a' dol mar àite-fèill le daoine às gach ceàrnaidh a' tadhal agus tha Anna toilichte aoigheachd a thoirt dhaibh agus comhairle nuair a bhios e dhìth. Tha a piuthar, Seonag, daonnan ri taobh ga cuideachadh agus a' toirt dhith taic. Tha Anna na ball làidir den phàrtaidh Libearalach.

Chìtear Anna gu tric a-muigh agus mun cuairt

taobh siar a' bhaile, a falt ruadh agus a h-aodach dathtach ga comharrachadh a-measg an t-sluaigh. Tha i na Crìosdaidh làidir aig a bheil mòran charaidean den h-uile seòrsa creud.

Tha an leabhar seo a' toirt dhuinn dealbh air leth, chan ann a-mhàin air eachdraidh beatha boireannach làidir inntinneach, ach air an dòigh-beatha a bha ann an Leòdhas ro àm a' chogaidh – dòigh-beatha a tha air a thoirt beò gu h-ealanta tro bhriathran an ùghdair.

Beathag Mhoireasdan

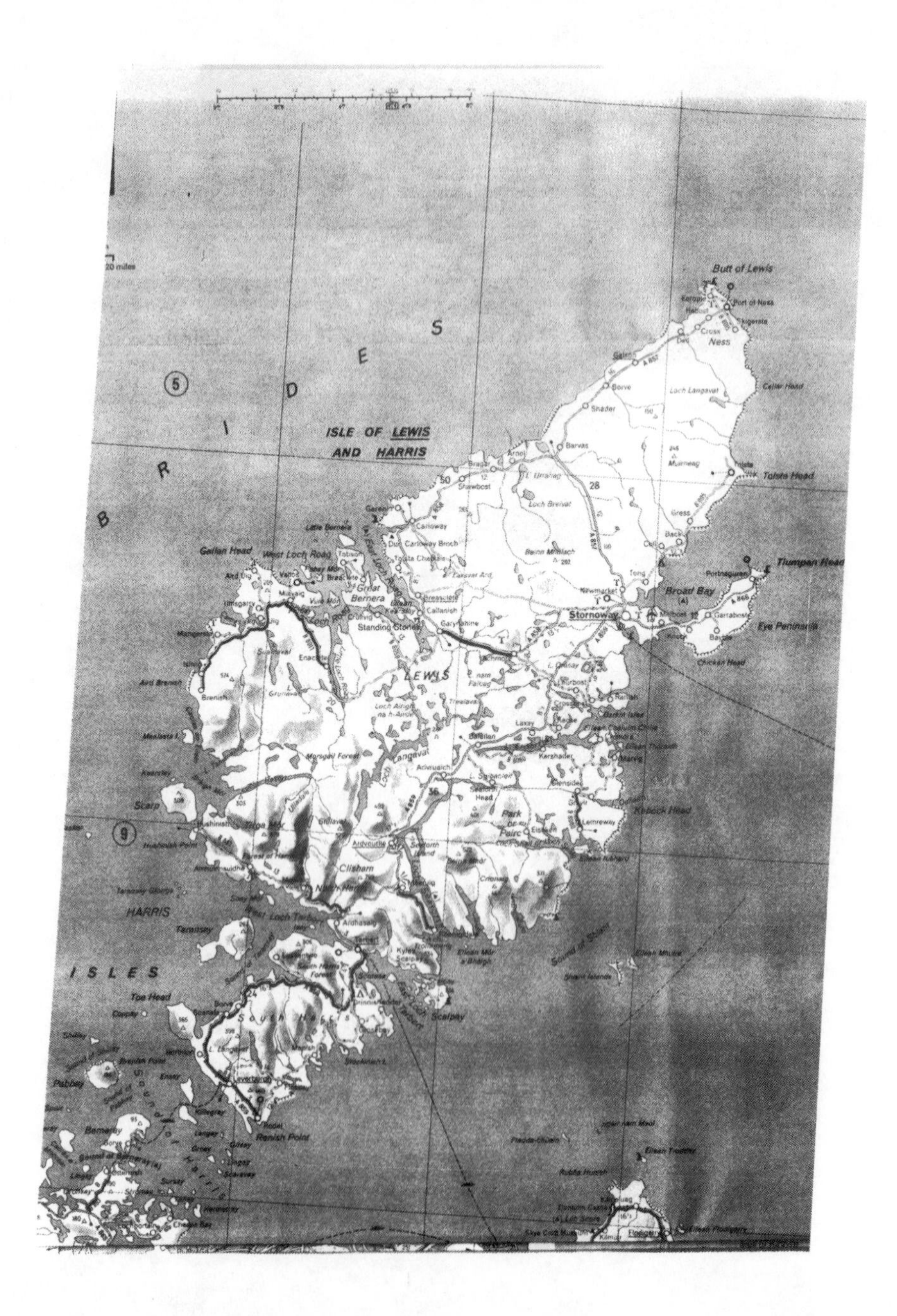

20 miles
Butt of Lewis
Port of Ness
Ness
Cellar Head
Loch Langavat
Barvas
Muirneag
Tolsta Head
Shawbost
Carloway
Dun Carloway Broch
Loch Breivat
Beinn Mholach
Tong
Tiumpan Head
Broad Bay
Stornoway
Newmarket
Eye Peninsula
Chicken Head
ISLE OF LEWIS
AND HARRIS
H E B R I D E S
5
Gallan Head
West Loch Roag
Great
Bernera
Callanish
Standing Stones
Garynahine
Uig
Brenish
Ardvourlie
Mangersta
LEWIS
Loch Langavat
Laxay
Kershader
Park
Kebock Head
Lemreway
Scarp
Clisham
North Harris
Sound of Shiant
Shiant Islands
Eilean Mhuire
HARRIS
Taransay
Toe Head
Tarbert
Scalpay
Leverburgh
Rodel
Renish Point
Pabbay
Berneray
Sound of Harris
Eilean Trodday
Flodigarry
9
ISLES

EARLY DAYS

Rugadh mise eader dà bhèile da chlò mòr !

Born between two bales of tweed !

That is what I was told by my dear aunt Christina Campbell, who was the first to visit Mother and me after my birth on 22nd December 1919. The Isle of Lewis is famous for its tweed, and Havelock Lane, Stornoway was lined with bales of the cloth. My aunt had to walk between them to reach the stairs leading to Number Twelve.

My mother Christina MacMillan had rented a room there since her marriage to my father, Donald Nicolson, in 1918. It cost her 4s 6d per week. Father, who was an Able Seaman in the Royal Navy, did not join her until he was demobbed in January 1919. He very nearly did not survive to join her at all because he boarded the ill-fated ship *Iolaire* to sail from Kyle of Lochalsh to Stornoway. The ship was full of Islanders happy to be going home after war service; many had been drinking and my non-smoking, tee-totaller father did not feel at ease among them. He decided to disembark and wait for the ordinary passenger ferry instead. This decision probably saved his life. The *Iolaire* was wrecked on a reef only a mile or so from Stornoway and just yards from the shore. One man managed to swim ashore with a line, and thanks to his efforts seventy-nine of those aboard were saved, including Neil Nicolson, my first cousin. But one hundred and eighty-one local men were drowned – having survived a World War, and so close to home!

Mother
The future Christina Nicolson as a young herring lassie at Peterhead

Father
Donald Nicolson on his croft. An ex-Royal Navy man who built his house at Orinsay

Their families had been airing their civilian clothes ready for their return. It was a terrible tragedy for the Island – all those bodies, young recruits and veteran sailors – laid out on the grass. But our family was one of the lucky ones, and so I was born in Stornoway in December 1919.

At about the time I was born, Lord Leverhulme arrived on the Island. He was one of the Lever Brothers who manufactured 'Sunlight Soap' across the Mersey from Liverpool. Lever's got their oil from Africa but there was concern that the supply was going to dry-up and he came to Stornoway where he hoped to start a fishing industry that would fulfil their needs.

He bought most of the Island and lived in Lewis Castle for about five years. Lord Leverhulme established a fishing industry in south Harris at the village of Leverburgh.

In 1922 he announced he was withdrawing and offered the whole of Lewis to the Islanders. The people of Stornoway accepted his offer but the country folk refused, thinking there was a catch. There is still a Stornoway Trust for the land and fishing industries.

In 1925 Lord Leverhulme died of pneumonia. His co-directors, having no interest in the fisheries, closed them.

My parents were both from the village of Lemreway, and they had known each other all their lives. If you ever visit Lemreway you will think it a delightful spot, with the houses strung out round a beautiful bay which is sheltered by an island called in Gaelic *Iubhaird* – 'Edward's Island' and the tradition is that Bonnie Prince Charlie (Charles Edward Stuart) hid there before fleeing to Skye. This was 'way back in

1745, after his defeat at Culloden.

To the Nicolsons and the Macmillans Lemreway was a place of exile, because their parents had been evicted from the inland village of Stemreway. It was the old story – clearing out people to make room for sheep. Even today Stemreway is famous for the quality of the grass. But these Late Victorian clearances were not as savage as the earlier ones, because sixteen of the families from Stemreway were offered crofts beside the sea. While the sheep were enjoying their new grazing, my great-grandparents trudged across the moor to Lemreway, leading my grandfather Callum by the hand, and carrying baby Murdo in a creel on his mother's back. They had to ford a swollen river before they arrived at Lemreway where their new homes were waiting for them.

After the War my father did not want to go back to sea full-time. While I was still very young, he and my mother decided to get a piece of land, and at the age of two and a half I moved with them some thirty-two miles to the remote village of Orinsay. Here my father and thirteen other crofters simply squatted on land belonging to the Eisken Estate. The Estate owners raised no objections, perhaps because they felt guilty about the way families had been cleared to make room for deer hunting and salmon fishing. The fourteen new crofters were all local men, more likely than not related to the folk who had been evicted a generation earlier.

While my mother and father opted for a hard life on the land in Lewis, dozens of other Islanders who had no jobs decided to travel to Canada in search of work. It was in 1923 that the *Metagama* sailed into Stornoway harbour – the biggest ship ever to berth there. When she set sail, she carried a total of 315 emigrants, 260 of them from Lewis. The quay was crowded with hundreds of friends and relations saying goodbye. The *Metagama* was the last of a whole fleet of ships which had sailed from the Hebrides laden with emigrants. I believe all the lads who sailed on her arrived safely in Canada, but the Islanders who had sailed on earlier ships were often not as lucky. Back in the 1880s my great-uncle Louis Nicolson had set off for Canada, but the poor man died at sea. Rumour had it that when the journey took longer than expected, there was not enough food to go round.

Christina Nicolson with daughters Anne (standing) and Cathy outside their hut at Orinsay (c1922)

My earliest memory is of walking to the tarred linen hut where the three of us were to live while father and his friends built a better house for the family.

It was behind a screen in that one-room hut that my mother gave birth to my brother, John, in 1926. She was attended by two amateur midwives – 'howdies' we called them – and the last thing she needed was an inquisitive child butting in. But Aunt Peggy, who kept a shop when she was not delivering babies, knew how to get rid of me. She threw a bag of sweeties over the screen and I left Mother alone.

In the winter my father used to fish for eels, and I remember he got a very nasty bite from one which got hold of his thumb and would not let go until he hacked its head off with a knife. The wound went septic, and I remember father pacing the floor, unable to sleep for the pain, while the poison, marked by a red line on his skin spread up his arm. Of course there was no penicillin in those days, and no doctor or chemist near to help. Father showed me how to make an oatmeal poultice – a big ball of oatmeal the size of a dumpling – to draw the poison. This was my introduction to nursing! The poultices worked, and the eel bite finally healed.

Unfortunately not all the old fashioned remedies were as effective as poultices. When I was a child – long before there were vaccines against measles – it was believed that it was a bad thing to drink water if you had the disease. Parents would dose their children with sulphur to 'bring out the spots' and get the illness over with. It so happened that my sister Cathy, brother John and I were suffering from measles when our grandmother Catriona Nicolson died. Our parents left us alone in the house and went off to the funeral. My brother John was desperate for water; he drank the contents of the stone hot water bottle that mother had left to keep him warm. As the eldest, I felt obliged to report him to my parents when they came home. Even then I was acting like a Matron!

There must have been a measles epidemic at the time. While we were recovering on sulphur, two people in the village died – a pregnant woman and her young daughter. The other daughter, Peggy Nicolson who survived, would later become my schoolmate. The shock of losing both wife and child turned Domhaill Ruidh (Red haired Donald) into a strict Christian.

BLACK HOUSES

You may have heard of 'black houses' in the Hebrides. My grandmother, Catriona Nicolson, lived in one. She had a peat fire in the middle of the floor, and a big hook hung above it to hold pots. Maybe it was the position of the house, I don't know, but most of the smoke went straight out the hole in the roof. Other black householders were not so lucky – some were permanently kippered by the peat-smoke which swirled around their home.

In my grandmother's house we ate in a separate room away from the fire. Here Granny kept a dresser covered in ornaments including a china doll which I coveted. "Eat up your food and you'll get the doll!" I was told. But one day a ram wandered into the house and knocked the doll off the dresser with his horn.

My grandmother's kitchen had another traditional feature besides the central fire – bed alcoves set in the stone wall. The old-fashioned bed was reckoned to be

Hole-in-the-wall bed

very cosy, and I am sure Grandma meant well when she settled my little sister and me there one night. But we were very young and restless. Poor Cathy fell out of the bed – which was much higher off the floor than a conventional cot – and hit her head on the stone flags. It was still sore the next night when we were back in our own home. Cathy cried and Mother spanked her for causing a fuss – she didn't realise that the wee soul was in pain! My grandfather had decided to keep shtum about the accident – he told us later that he would have kept quiet about Cathy's fall even if she had died!

MY FATHER'S WHITE HOUSE

Our new home was a 'white house' where the fire burned in a conventional fireplace. It was so grand compared to the hut – it had two bedrooms upstairs for the children, and downstairs my parents' room, living room, kitchen, and bathroom. My father, who was very good with his hands, built most of the house himself, though he had to hire a stonemason to erect the gable ends. The fireplace lintel was simply a boulder that Father and two of my uncles had found on the moor and lugged back to the house. They fitted it themselves. I took all this for granted – what stuck in my mind was the laugh when my uncle's bonnet fell into a pail of water. I was very proud of carrying my own little stool by its finger hole to our new white house (as shown on the back cover). That was in the mid-20s.

I soon forgot what little English I had learnt in Stornoway, and spoke nothing but Gaelic until I went to school, aged five. Even at that age I was expected to walk the two miles to school along a rough road. No wonder we children often arrived wet and dishevelled! But we had a kind, Gaelic-speaking teacher called Bellann. She made sure we were dried at the classroom fire, and gave us cocoa each day at 11.00. This was supposed to be a treat for us, but I didn't enjoy it and I have never liked cocoa since. My first day at school was a happy one – I was given a slate and told to draw someone I knew. My portrait of our neighbour 'Butler' with huge head and tiny body made our teacher laugh because in reality 'Butler' was a big burly man with a small head. That was my first taste of education, and ever since I have enjoyed learning new things.

My grandparents lived near the school, and I usually had lunch with them, tatties and herring or home-made soup. At that time nearly all our food – except the cocoa – was produced locally. Everyone kept sheep. The young ewes were kept for breeding, but most of the ram lambs were slaughtered and their meat salted. Of course there were no deep freezes in those days. Some Lewis folk – mostly those living near Ness – would hunt the seabird with the Gaelic name 'gugha' and eat them. However I can't tell you what they taste like because my family never touched these birds. Most country people had a cow, and the milk they did not drink was churned into butter or made into crowdie cheese. Looking back, I am very grateful that I had such a good diet as a child. Mind you, if I had been one of many folk allergic to dairy products, I would not have thrived as I did.

DALLAS'S OF COWCADDENS

On the Island we had no shops to buy fancy clothes, and so most people ordered clothes from catalogues supplied by firms such as Oxendales, JD Williams – still trading in 2002! – and Dallas's of Cowcaddens (in Glasgow). I remember the day when my sister Cathy and I were left alone in the house while Mother and Father were out cutting peats. I suppose modern parents would be afraid to do that in case they were reported to the Social Work Department. Somehow Cathy managed to drop the precious Dallas catalogue into the open fire, and I could not save it. I ran outside screaming.

When Father heard me he flung down his peat-iron in alarm, maybe thinking that Cathy had hurt herself. But when he learnt that the only casualty was the mail-order catalogue, he told me to be quiet. The ever-obliging Dallas's quickly sent a replacement and I thought no more about the episode until I returned from Africa in 1966, and learnt that the real Dallas's store had been destroyed by fire. By that time Stornoway had some proper shops, and there was not the same demand on Lewis for mail order goods.

THE FISHING

Father had not given up the sea altogether. As well as working the croft, he sailed regularly with a group of men who had a fishing boat – *The Kebbock Head* – berthed at Lemreway, the village where he had been born. All week the men fished, taking the catch back to Stornoway each day to sell. On Saturday they all went home to spend Sunday with their families. We looked forward to Father walking home on Saturday night with a bagful of herring for us. Mother gutted them and often put them out to dry in the sun. The herring were not smoked like kippers, just dried in the fresh air. These were delicious fried, even nicer than fresh herring, and they turned a lovely red colour in the pan. But we had to watch the seagulls, otherwise they would have stolen all the fish before they were dry!

Fishing Boats at Stornoway

SUNDAY

After working hard for six days, my parents were only too glad to spend Sunday in a different way. We all walked three miles across the moor to the Free Church at Gravir. The roads were bad, but it would have been unthinkable not to go. Of course, after the service we had to walk back home again, and then my parents would retire to bed for a well-earned rest – as much of a rest as they could get with five children charging about. The Free Church disapproved of children playing on a Sunday, but we had so much energy, even after walking six miles over the moors, that we still jumped around.

THE EASY WAY TO GET ABOUT

Because the roads on Lewis were so bad, many people preferred to use boats to get from one part of the Island to another. For instance, back in 1916 a young married couple set out from Stornoway. The husband, Callum McLeod, wanted to get to Lemreway to introduce his Islay-born wife Flora to his family. They hitched a ride on a fishing boat which was heading for Lemreway Bay to anchor for the weekend. Because it was the end of the season all the crew had had a good drink, and Callum joined them. Drunk or not, they arrived safely in the Bay and struggled up a steep hill to the McLeods' thatched cottage.

This was not only a black house – fire in the middle of the floor – but an actual 'but and ben' with the beasts occupying the left side of the building while the people lived on the right. Donald McLeod was expecting them and the party continued until late into the night. Eventually the old man retired into the other room, leaving the honeymoon couple to sleep in the hole in the wall bed. There was a pile of fresh straw for them to lie on – not even in a tick mattress – just covered by a sheet. Callum fell sound asleep right away, but Flora lay awake. Suddenly she felt the bedding pulled from under her. One of the cows had broken loose from her stall and decided to help herself to some of the honeymoon couple's straw. The blushing bride had to be rescued by her father-in-law, who hauled the cow back to its own side of the cottage and tied it up again.

It was more than twenty years after this incident that my sister Cathy got the offer of work at the Eiskin Estate Lodge. She was asked to teach the children of the Estate workers. Though Eiskin was only some five miles from Orinsay, the land route was so rough that Cathy could scarcely have walked it, especially as she had only just been discharged from hospital. Once again, the solution was to travel by sea. My father offered to take her to work each Monday in his boat, and to collect her on Fridays so that she could spend the weekend at home.

One Friday Father came to pick up Cathy as usual, and they sailed back to Orinsay. On the Saturday morning, Cathy was amazed to discover her pet cat, Sally, in the family barn. She had left Sally comfortably installed at Eisken, but for some unknown reason the cat had decided to follow her. The poor little animal must have run along the shore as her mistress travelled by sea. It was a miracle that Sally had not got lost on the way or drowned in a rock pool. Having made this epic journey, Sally decided to stay at Orinsay. Cathy later tried to persuade her to settle in the village of Uig where she taught next, but the pupils teased Sally so she retired to Orinsay for good.

Looking back on the start of Cathy's career in education, it seems incredible that anyone could have considered teaching a suitable job for a young girl who was in delicate health! These days it is not only cats that are tormented by school children. But Cathy was a great success as a teacher and she continued to work with children for the next forty-odd years.

MY SECONDARY SCHOOL

When I was about ten I left the primary class and joined the class run by the Headmaster, who was a very able teacher, but strict. He would give us what he called 'extra-curricular activities' – for example he had us staging mock elections. We could choose to vote for Ramsay MacDonald, who was the Labour Prime Minister, or Moffat Pender, Conservative. My father told me to vote for Ramsay MacDonald, which I did. One of the other pupils decided to support Moffat Pender – not a popular choice! From that time until the day he died, sixty years later, he was nicknamed 'Moffat'.

Maybe it was the Viking tradition, but everyone on Lewis got a nickname from early childhood. One wee lad turned up at school wearing a multi-coloured cape – that earned him the nickname of 'Joseph'. Because I was interested in nursing from primary school days, dressing up in a wee white cap, the other children dubbed me 'Sister Annie' – hence the name of this book.

Lewis people of my generation were strongly

discouraged from talking Gaelic at school. This was not done to stop us being cheeky to the teachers – both our primary school teacher and the excellent Headmaster were native speakers themselves. They made us speak English all the time at school to help us get on in the world outside the Hebrides. It may seem harsh, but it was done with the best of intentions. Of course, at home and in the village of Orinsay we all spoke Gaelic. My father made sure that I could read the language by sitting with me on his knee each Sunday night. I would read the Gaelic Bible, and he would correct my pronunciation. Thanks to his efforts I am able to read Gaelic as well as speak it, though I must admit that my spelling leaves a lot to be desired.

As I said, we had to walk two miles to and from school. Getting wet was not the only problem. In those days – and until very recently – bulls roamed freely over the Island. Most of the time they were too busy with the cows to bother us, but sometimes children would tease the bulls and get chased for a few yards. Our route to school lay along the side of a fresh water loch. When this froze in the winter-time we were warned to stay off the ice, but as you can imagine it was a magnet to us. I know of one Lewis boy who drowned while playing on a frozen loch. In bad weather my father or one of the other crofters would come to meet us from school, Bbt if the weather was fine we children would be expected to take things to our grandparents in Lemeray. I remember one time walking the two miles to school with a clucking hen. This was destined for my grandmother Nicolson, who had eggs for the hen to sit on.

Strong winds blow on Lewis all the year round, but only in the wildest weather were we allowed to miss school. My brother John was only too happy to stay at home, but I liked school and I tried to go every day. If the wind was strong, we would open our coats like wings and try to fly down the road!

The Headmaster at our little school did his very best for us, but of course there was no way he could give us the sort of education we would have had at the Nicolson Institute in Stornoway. If only my parents had stopped in the Island capital instead of going to their tarred hut in Orinsay, I could perhaps have attended University instead of leaving school at fourteen.

The Nicolson Institute took its name from a Lewisman, Alexander Nicolson, who was killed in an explosion aboard ship in Shanghai. Though he was only a young man, he had had the foresight to make a will leaving his modest savings to found a school on his native Island. His surviving brothers, who were scattered over the world, clubbed together to provide the money to carry out Alexander's bequest. The school flourished and since 1873 has produced many distinguished scholars. Yet its very success has led to the most able Islanders leaving Lewis to find posts elsewhere.

I DECIDE TO BECOME A MENTAL NURSE

Though I had taken an interest in my father's home remedies and played at being a nurse, it was at the age of nine that my future career was decided. One of our neighbours in Orinsay, a lad of eighteen, got into an argument with older men. One of the men punched him on the temple, and I think this must have caused a hematoma (blood clot) in the parietal region of his brain. Certainly from that day forward the poor boy was never right. His mother eventually got to hear about the scrap with the older man, but by then it was too late to have her son taken to the nearest hospital in Stornoway. All that summer he ran wild, never getting down to any proper work and – strangely – refusing to eat in his own house. He feared he was being poisoned. His father tried to help the young man by getting him a job as cook aboard the boat which he sailed on, but after his first fishing trip it was clear that there was something seriously wrong with him.

At last his parents decided to call a doctor, who could only reach the village by riding his motorbike through mud as thick as porridge. The lad refused to be examined in his own home, and after the briefest of consultations in a cousin's house, the doctor had him committed to the asylum in Inverness. One signature was all it took – one doctor's signature and half a crown for his fee. Schizophrenia was diagnosed; sufferers often believe they are being poisoned.

I still shudder to think of the way that poor lad was taken to hospital. He must have spotted a boat coming from the Estate and guessed he was to be taken away. He made for the moor and I wondered if he was heading for a loch to drown himself. I alerted my father and along with the other men, he went after the lad and persuaded him to come quietly to the boat where he was tied up with enormous thick mooring ropes. As the boat drew away from the beach, he shouted to his mother: "Mammy! Will I ever see you again?" He never did.

He was taken trussed like that to Lemreway where he was transferred – still tied up – to another boat that was to take him to Stornoway where he was loaded on to the passenger boat to Kyle of Lochalsh. I don't think anyone would have bothered to give him food or a hot drink on the journey which took at least eight hours. People were frightened of mental patients; some of the poor Islanders treated in this way died before they reached the asylum. The young man died three years later and returned home in his coffin.

As the poor lad was taken away from Orinsay, I stood behind my father. I said: "I think his mother is poisoning him without meaning to." This remark did not go down well with my parents, who thought I was taking an unhealthy interest in our neighbour's misfortune. But I never forgot this young man, and it was his illness that inspired me to become a psychiatric nurse and later to study allergies and the way they can exacerbate mental problems. However it was to be another nine years before I was able to start nursing training.

FUN AND GAMES

From about the age eleven or twelve, I loved to go to the dancing. No Palais for us – the young people of Lewis gathered on a convenient stretch of road to dance! One of the boys had a melodeon – a small accordion – and we did all the Scottish country-dances. My parents would not have approved of me going off like that and mixing with boys, so I had to give an excuse such as having to go to post a letter. My good friend Sophie Kennedy would join me and we would enjoy ourselves for a couple of hours until it was time for us to go home. On one occasion when we were merrily road dancing, I spotted my father, who had unexpectedly come off the boat. He was walking home, but Sophie and I ran like hares to get home before him. As soon as I got home I jumped into bed. "I could swear I saw Ann and Sophie running down the road ahead of me," Father said. But Mother assured him that I had been in bed for a while.

As I said before, the sudden loss of his wife and child had turned Domhaill Ruaidh into a very strict Christian. This meant that he often left his daughter Peggy alone at home while he went off to services in the next village. Once Peggy became a teenager her home was popular as a 'ceilidh house' – a place where villagers young and old got together to sing and play music. Everyone would gather in the kitchen. Nobody ever ventured into the dining room, the place where Peggy's mother and sister had died years before. There would be a lot of pranks and carryings on – nothing nasty, just youthful high spirits, like putting a traffic cone on Donald Dewar's statue today. Some of the boys would swing the oil lanterns – Lewis's answer to the disco ball!

As the night wore on, the lads would take turns to watch outside for the return of Peggy's father. In theory he could be spotted on the skyline, well before he got close enough to hear the music coming from his house. But one night the watchers must have missed his silhouette and he got almost to the front door before the party realised he was home. Everyone scattered. Some of the lads who hadn't had time to escape dived into the left hand side of the cottage – the old cow byre – and hid there. But when Peggy's father burst in he chased them round the herring barrels. He was in a rare mood for it!

Poor Domhaill Ruaidh! Only a month after the tragic drowning of Murdo Kennedy, he perished in another fishing accident at the other end of the Bay. He and three other men had gone out in a sailing boat to lift the nets. The weather was stormy and perhaps a gust of wind knocked the sail out of control. Whatever happened they were all thrown into the sea. Domhaill Ruaidh, a strong swimmer, reached the shore. But when he realised that his brother Angus was still in the water, he went back to rescue him. He succeeded in getting Angus ashore, and then bravely went back to try to help the other two fishers. All three drowned. This tragedy left Peggy an orphan. When she eventually married she left the village for Balallan. I was relieved when the old ceilidh house was later demolished and a nephew of Domhaill Ruaidh built a lovely bungalow on the site. Every time I saw the old cottage I was reminded of the tragedies associated with it.

LIFE ON A PRE – WAR CROFT

Living on a croft, we all worked from an early age. One of my first tasks was to scrape the lichen, called crotal, from the rocks and bring it home to dye the wool from our sheep. Crotal turned the wool a lovely rusty red colour, but I think my parents valued it mainly because gathering the stuff kept us out from under their feet for hours.

One of the differences between sheep rearing in the Lowlands and what crofters do, is that in the Highlands rams run with the ewes all year round, instead of being penned separately. Left to themselves, sheep are very much like human beings and they will

Sheep Farming

make babies at any time of year, but it is much better from the crofters' point of view if mating takes place in September so that the lambs are born in April when the winter is past. Young ewes particularly are very enthusiastic, and so to make sure that they did not fall pregnant at the wrong time of year, crofters would issue them with contraceptive patches! Father would find a spare piece of cloth and painstakingly stitch it over the young ewe's backside, so that even the randiest ram could not impregnate her. These rags, 'luideag' in Gaelic, are still used in the Islands, and visitors are often surprised to see the flocks of sheep with brightly coloured rumps grazing the hills.

When September came around, crofters would often import a ram from outside the village to cover the ewes. This was partly to prevent inbreeding, but also to improve the flock and get a higher percentage of females. Rams that had the name of making a lot of ewe lambs were in great demand. To make sure that the imported ram didn't tire himself out fighting, all the other males were rounded up and taken to an offshore island. My father and brother had some close shaves transporting boisterous rams in a small open boat. Maybe the beasts knew that they were going to miss out on all the fun!

In the summer, maybe early May, all the sheep and their lambs were brought in from the moor. The adult sheep were tied up in fanking pens and sheared. Both men and women wielded the clippers. You had to be careful not to nick the sheep's skin when you were cutting the wool, which was always full of twigs and dirt. Once the worst of the debris had been cleaned from the fleeces, they were dyed. We would build a fire on the banks of the burn near our house, set a big pot on the peats and put in layers of wool, each well sprinkled with crotal. The pot would simmer for maybe two hours.

Once the wool had been dyed, it was dried on the fence and then carded into little plaits. These plaits were then fed into the spinning wheel. I remember my mother spinning our wool using the old-fashioned wheel – I stuck my finger into the spokes, and howled when I got hurt!

The finished yarn was sent off to Stornoway to be woven into tweed. But even then there was work to be done on it – the cloth was sent back to Orinsay to be 'waulked' or worked into the standard 28" width. As recently as the 1930s when I was a schoolgirl this was done in the traditional way, with five or six females on each side of the tweed. We would sing Gaelic songs to keep our rhythm. My mother stood at the foot of the table with a measure to make sure we got the width right. Though only women waulked the cloth, these sessions were great social events. The young men would drop by to see the talent – the good looking young girls – and they would stay for a cup of tea and a chat.

Potatoes were an important crop, and we were trained to cut up the seed potatoes carefully so as to get as many new plants as possible. Father would dig the furrow or trench, we children would place the bits of tuber on the ground and then mother would put cow manure on top before shovelling on the earth. In the 1930s it was considered a poor show to use seaweed as fertiliser, though it had served earlier generations of Islanders well.

Though my parents took a very practical view of dumb creatures, – killing their own sheep, sending cattle for slaughter – from a very early age I loved animals for themselves. I cried my eyes out when one of our black cows was sold to the butcher. Not many Islanders are so soft hearted, yet even tough crofters could find themselves with pet animals. Those motherless lambs reared in the kitchen would return to the house, even when they were grown sheep, and walk in like long-lost cousins.

PREMONITIONS & WARNINGS

Though my father was deeply religious, both he and my mother believed that you could tell where a tragedy was going to occur some time in the future by seeing signs. One of the most common warnings of death was a light like a flame, seen where no fire was burning. The first time I saw such a warning 'Teine Biorach' was when I was a girl of nine or ten. Looking out from the house at Orinsay, my Montgomery cousins showed me flames that seemed to run up and down from a boat moored on the other side of the bay. Some of the flames ran right up the hill overlooking the mooring. My mother was not pleased. Though the Montgomeries were our cousins, she did not approve of the way they all seemed to have 'the second sight' and she did not want them to encourage a child like me to see such things.

Meanwhile across the sea from Orinsay, in the Estate Deer Park, there was a hut where wardens would watch out for deer poachers. Many folk who stayed in this hut heard awful crashing noises in the night. It was years later, during World War II, that a plane crashed over that hut. Because the crash site was so remote, it was six weeks before the bodies of the crew were recovered. Wrapped in tarpaulin, the dead were brought to Orinsay and then put on a boat at the same spot as my cousins and I had seen the flames years before.

We thought that the loss of the plane would mean the end of the 'Teine Biorach', but the strange flames continued to burn until February 1945, when another tragedy occurred near this spot. Four local men had been fishing for herring. It seems that when they went to lift the nets at 6.00am, there was such a weight of fish that the boat went down, drowning Louis MacMillan, the owner of the boat, and another older fisherman. It seems the two men were caught in their own nets and pulled under. A young sailor who had been helping that night succeeded in getting clear of the boat and swam towards the rocks, hoping to climb to safety. But strong as he was he could not pull off both his seaboots. He managed to get free of one, but then he fell back into the sea and he too drowned.

The fourth man, Murdo Kennedy, who was in his sixties, clung to the boat. Neither his body nor the wreck of the boat were ever found. After the tragedy his wife described what had happened just before he left to join the fishers. As he ate his breakfast and she warmed his cravat at the fire, Murdo told his wife of a dream where he stood before a king who put a crown on his head. She believed that this dream had been a premonition that he would meet the King of Glory that very day. Murdo Kennedy, who belonged to a well-known Island family, was a strict Christian. His son, Callum Kennedy, became a famous singer.

The 'Teine Biorach' was not seen on the shore again after the loss of the four fishermen.

'Tigh a Bhodaich' – House of the Old Man – is the name given to a landmark on the road to Stornoway. Fires like the one I described have been seen there for

In The Western Isles by G.W. Lennox Patterson

years, and only last year two young men were killed at that spot when their car left the road.

Other premonitions were more personal. I nursed my father during the last month of his life. We slept in the same room so that I could attend to him. During the night I heard nothing, but he would say to me' "What a time those children are having up the stairs!" "Whose children are they?" I would ask, knowing perfectly well we were alone. He insisted that my sister Joan's children were on holiday in the house.

On the day Father died, my other sister came home with her two younger children, who did indeed make a noise in the room above where their grandfather had lain. One of the youngsters fell out of bed, directly above the coffin laid out in the room below. My auntie went upstairs to quieten the wee ones. I said to her, "He (Father) has heard all this before!"

In 1977 my sister Cathy spent a holiday in Motherwell with me and my husband Rankine. We were having lunch before going shopping in Callander with my other sister. Rankine had been listening to the radio and when the news was finished, he switched off. Suddenly we all heard a sound like an announcement from the big extractor fan above the cooker. It took us by surprise and we could not catch the words. Then there was a loud slam like the lid of an old-fashioned radiogram closing. Rankine checked the radio, though he knew he had switched it off. He sat quiet, cutting up his dinner, and eyeing the extractor fan. I felt uneasy all day, even when we were in Callander at the mill shop.

Two days later Cathy went home, but she was to return to Motherwell nine days later for Rankine's funeral. He suffered a massive coronary and died before I could call for help. When the ambulance arrived, the paramedics called the hospital to have an emergency bed prepared for a cardiac arrest case. One of our neighbours heard the message and came to see if he could help me. I believe that the 'announcement' we had all heard at lunchtime was a premonition of this call to the hospital.

Most Island people had some experience of premonitions, though some like the Montgomeries were more susceptible than others. But I soon learnt not to talk about such things to sceptical mainland folk. Years later when I was in Uganda and Kenya, I could well understand why the Africans would not discuss their beliefs with foreigners.

RELIGION

While I was growing up on Lewis, most Island people were members of the Free Church to which our whole family belonged. As I have described, it was the done thing to walk three miles to the Sunday service and three miles home again, dressed in your best, no matter how wild the weather. In the year I started nursing in Glasgow, 1938, there was a terrific Religious Revival in Lewis. It started at Garyvard, a village several miles from Orinsay, while Duncan Campbell of the Faith Mission was preaching. I know one of the people who was present at the first service, a divinity student called Kenneth Nicolson. Immediately afterwards he had to leave Lewis to preach himself in Rosehall, Sutherland, though he would have dearly loved to stay at home and enjoy the spiritual awakening. He wrote a lovely song in Gaelic to express his feelings, leaving the warmth of the revival for his duty as a student minister.

An Tèid thu Leam a Ghearraidh-bhàrd?

An tèid thu leam a Ghearraidh-Bhàrd
Far bheil Spiorad naomh nan Gràs
Ri toirt muinntir dh'ionnsaigh slàinte
Sa staigh fo sgàil na brataiche
An tèid thu leam a Ghearraidh-Bhàrd

Nuair a chuala mise an sgeul
Bha mo shùil a' sileadh dheur
'S cha be bròn a lìon mo chrè
Ach gràdh bha 'n èiginn bheannaichte
An tèid thu leam a Ghearraidh-Bhàrd

Take me to Garyvard

Will you take me to Garyvard –
Where I will find the spirit of love
Which brings people back to health
And under the shadow of the banner
Will you take me to Garyvard?

When I heard the news
I shed tears but it was not sorrow
That filled my heart, but love
That was in blessed need.
Will you take me to Garyvard?

The next year, 1939, another revival began, this time in the Free Church Mission House at the village of Lemreway. The preacher on this occasion was a first cousin of Father – Callum MacMillan – who was a great orator. All of a sudden people, men as well as women, began to faint. They had to be carried outside and laid on the grass. This led to suspicions that the 'revival' was just hysteria. I can assure you that many Islanders who had gone to church just for the sake of appearances became wonderful Christians at this time. Many of the people who discovered their faith in 1939 remained good-living believers until their dying day. Jessie McRitchie, a school friend of mine, was one of those converted in 1939 at the age of sixteen. She died aged only twenty-six in the Stornoway Sanatorium, another victim of TB. But before she passed away she wrote several hymns and a beautiful song describing how she had become a Christian.

Jessie's Hymn

'S e na buachaillean a chual' am fuaim an toiseach
Bha iad faire air an treud, bha duais 'ga feitheamh
Shoillsich bho nèamh orr' reult na maidne.
Sgap na neòil roimh chumhachd Iehòbha.

Bho rugadh an t-uan bha buaidh 'ga leantainn
Ged bha sgàil air a ghlòir, 'na fhe òl cha robh peacadh.
Bha cumhachd na cheum do'n ghèill an talamh -
'S e bh' ann dara pearsa na mòrachd.

The shepherds first heard the sound
Tending their flock, a prize awaited them. From the heavens
On them shone the light of morning
And the heavens opened before the power of Jehovah.

From the birth of the Lamb, success followed him.
Although there was a shadow on his glory, in his flesh there was no sin.
There was power in his step, to which the earth yielded.
He was the second person of the Blessed Trinity.

THE BARVAS REVIVAL

Some twelve years later in 1950 there was another powerful Revival, starting this time in the village of Barvas. By the 1950s many Islanders had tape recorders, and so there is a record of the testimonies of the later generation of converts. But sadly there is no audio record of those amazing years, 1938 to 1939, when the revival was sweeping the District of Lochs.

WORK

I got my first paid job when I was thirteen and still at school. In the summer holidays our next door neighbour 'Butler' – the fat man with the small head – recruited twenty-odd girls from Orinsay and the surrounding villages to work for a week on Eisken Estate. We all stayed together in the Gillies' House – great fun! – and each day went to the moors to carry

Anne Nicolson sets off to work the peats (1933) Despite appearances it was good fun

Peat Cutters

peats to the roadside. Good old Butler did his best to spin out the work for us, and I earned twenty-five shillings, which was enough to buy a pair of smart new shoes and a lovely blue coat with a fur collar.

LERWICK ADVENTURE

Foreigners looking at the map of Scotland may assume that the islands scattered round the north and west of the country are all much the same. Nothing could be further from the truth. The Norse settlers who came to Lewis in the ninth century were entirely absorbed by the natives, though a lot of Norse words survive in our dialect of Gaelic. But in the Orkney and

Shetland Islands the Norse tradition prevailed. A version of old Norse was spoken on these islands until recent times, and their way of life was – and still is – very different from that on Lewis, where most people belong to the Free Church.

You can imagine then, how alarmed my parents were in 1936 when, aged sixteen, I begged for permission to join two pals who were off to Lerwick to work as herring gutters. The plan was that we would be away for eight weeks at the height of the fishing season. The prospect of toiling twelve hours a day did not deter me at all – I could easily work as hard at home on the croft – and I was desperate to earn some real money. Our board and lodgings would be provided and so the wages we earned would be pure profit. My parents reluctantly agreed to let me go, but I was well warned not to talk to any coopers. Why my mother and father thought the coopers were a bigger threat to innocent young girls than fishermen or the sailors based on Shetland I don't know.

Coopers

I begged for a new suitcase to take my bits and pieces to Lerwick, and eventually I was given one. But first I had a terrible scare – an aunt offered me the use of a basket which had originally contained suet, and which carried the butcher's name: 'ROBERT ALLAN, DINGWALL' in big black letters on the outside. If I had had to take that monstrosity with me I would have given up all thoughts of Lerwick. I was not allowed to wear the lovely blue coat I had bought from the peat money, but my uncle and his wife gave me a nice beige outfit with side pleats and slim lapels. In those days you had to wear a hat to go anywhere, and so a rat-coloured velour cloche completed my outfit.

Though he must have been worried about me, my dear father did not want to spoil our adventure. Before I left Stornoway, he took me to *The Kebbock Head*, let me rest for a couple of hours, and then gave me a good feed of herring, rolls and fishermen's biscuits before I joined my friends on the boat to Kyle.

As the crow flies, it is about 380km from Stornoway to Lerwick, but to get there we had to sail across the Minch, then take the bus to Aberdeen and then sail overnight to the Shetlands – maybe twice as far! By the time we arrived, my teenage pals and I looked sick, and we were nearly sent home again as unfit for the hard work on the quay. I don't know how I would have lived down the disgrace if I had returned home empty-handed.

We began work at eight o'clock in the morning. Kirsty-Mary and I cut open the herring and cleaned them before handing them over to the third member of the crew, a big girl called Dollog, who packed them tightly bones and all in barrels of salt.

After I had been in Lerwick about a fortnight, I was approached by one of the coopers I had been warned against. Looking back, I am sure the poor man was only doing his job supervising our work, but I got flustered, and gashed my hand with the gutting knife. You can still see the scar on my right pinkie to this day. By the weekend the cut was no better and so I was told to report to the First Aid Post run by the Mission to Seamen. The volunteers were so kind. They dressed my wound and offered me a cup of tea. But I refused, because it was Sunday and the Free Kirk did not allow tea drinking after church. Looking back I laugh at my innocence, but memories of that incident help me understand why strict Muslims who come to my house will not take any food or drink because it is not halal.

My eight weeks in Lerwick earned me the sum of £8.00 which was enough to let me buy presents for all the family. In those days all the women wore cotton overalls about the house, and so I bought them all overalls costing one shilling and eleven pence each.

My own special outfit was a lovely brown suit with a light brown straw hat and an umbrella. In those days 'Sunday Best' meant something. You were expected to dress up specially to attend church, and that is why my mother insisted on the coat I had bought from my peat money and the new brown suit being reserved for Sundays. It was so frustrating to see your best clothes hanging out of reach, going out of fashion.

GLASGOW HERE I COME

Shortly after my triumphant return from Lerwick, I got talking to an older girl, Nellie, who was home on holiday from Glasgow. She worked as a dining room maid, and she assured me she could get me a post as housemaid with the same family. We set off together, and when we arrived in Glasgow Nellie's sister, Annie, who worked for a well-off Jewish family, met us. She entertained me to the very first ice cream I had ever had in my life. It was 1936 and I was sixteen and a half years of age.

My new home was a big house in the West End of Glasgow, Kelvin Drive. There were three of us female servants, a very jolly woman who acted as cook for £3 a month, Nellie the table maid commanding £2.50 and me, the housemaid, on the lowest rate of £2.00. Some weekends we were free from six in the evening on Saturday until two o'clock on Sunday afternoon. When we had a Saturday night off, Nellie and I would head for the City Centre and *The Hielander's Umbrella* – the stretch of Argyle Street covered by the Central Station bridge. Here crowds of folk from the North – mostly young folk from the Islands – would meet up. The chat was all in Gaelic. Some old drunks would walk up and down with scruffy bagpipes. They didn't play much – people would pay them to keep quiet and move on. Sometimes lads would strike matches near these beggars hoping to light the meths fumes spouting from their pipes. Boys we met would often offer to see us home, but if we didn't like the look of them we would dodge off and jump on a tram without them.

Saturday night was the time for the *Hielander's Umbrella*, but if we had a Sunday evening to ourselves, we would go to the part of Great Western Road opposite what is now the Grosvenor Hotel, and once again there would be a crowd of young Islanders looking for company.

NURSING AT LAST

I had to wait until I was eighteen before I could start the nursing course I had set my heart on. I did correspondence classes in English and Arithmetic, so when I was old enough I was able to pass the entrance examination for nurse training. But passing the exams was not enough. All would-be nurses were interviewed, and had to demonstrate a good knowledge of current affairs. It would have been fatal to my hopes of becoming a nurse if the Sister-Tutor had learnt that I had been working as a housemaid! I had to pretend I was fresh off the Island of Lewis.

I chose to study Psychiatric Nursing because I hoped to help people like the local boy who had died in Inverness Asylum. I began my training at Hawkhead Psychiatric Hospital (now known as Leverndale) on 1st August 1938. I successfully completed three years of training, and after passing my Finals I qualified in 1941 as a Registered Psychiatric Nurse.

GENERAL NURSING

Next I applied to train as a General Nurse at the Eastern General Hospital in Duke Street, Glasgow. Of course we were in the middle of the War. The windows of the hospital were painted blue and there were heavy blackout blinds to stop any light leaking out to guide enemy airplanes.

I had barely started medical lectures before I was left in charge of a ward of about thirty patients at night. A more experienced nurse acted as a Runner – going from ward to ward at night to see how the trainees were managing. I was very anxious, particularly about a seriously ill old man in the top bed. I told myself that if he died on my shift I would run away. As I was giving out drugs from the cabinet in the middle of the ward, a patient said to me: "Move out the way of the hearse!" I could see that he was hallucinating, but there was nothing I could do for him at that point. One of the younger men in the ward, who was suffering from sciatic fever (a form of rheumatism) complained of an awful singing noise in his ears. Once again I lacked the experience to be able to help him.

The old man I had been worried about did indeed die in the night. The runner nurse helped me wash and dress him for his last journey. The porters came to move him to the mortuary.

As well giving nursing care to the thirty-odd patients, I was required to sort the dirty laundry, to count every item and to pack it up for collection in the morning. In a side ward there were four old men, segregated from the main ward because they were restless and noisy. I was expected to change, clean up and feed them all before the Sister came on duty in the morning. No question of delegating the chore to an auxiliary! As nurse-on-duty I was expected to do it all – a marathon job. Often I was so busy on night-duty that I had no time to prepare the food I had brought from the kitchen.

The Sister who was responsible for the ward was very strict, but I had great respect for her because she was so experienced and efficient. She would come on duty at 8.00 am and immediately read the Report Book. She ran her finger down the list of patients and listened carefully to my comments on each of them. When I reported the remark about the hearse, Sister calmly said: "He was drinking over New Year and he has DTs" (delirium tremens). Next I mentioned the sciatic fever patient and his complaints about a singing in his ears. Immediately Sister connected this symptom to his medication. "We have over-aspirined him" she said. "We'll change the dose today." And she was right too.

Each morning the Sister would speak to every single patient on the ward. A creature of habit, she would always stand on the patient's left side. I made sure that I always attended to the left side of the beds myself, leaving the other side to the patient who helped me out. It was a point of honour with the patients not to ask for bedpans during the Sister's round. As well as taking a keen interest in all medical developments, the Sister made sure that all the patients were clean and neatly dressed. Woe betide the nurse who presented a patient in a dirty shirt or one missing a button!

As a trainee general nurse I often found myself on night duty for a month or more at a stretch. We were entitled to a few nights off – maybe three per month – but the hospital would never give us more than a day or two's notice. We were afraid to ask when our time off was due, much as we were looking forward to it. At that time, 1942/43, the Polish Club at Charing Cross had a tremendous reputation, and my friends and I were keen to visit, but because we had to be back in the Nurses' Home by 10pm (even on our night off!) we never did get there.

However tired we were after a night on the ward, we trainees were expected to report for breakfast at eight o'clock, and then go on to a lecture and perhaps a tutorial after that. I remember one occasion when a young nurse sitting at the top end of the bench fell asleep and knocked the rest of us off the other end. Dr. Rogan of Stobhill gave our medical lectures and it says a lot for his teaching that we learnt so much despite being exhausted. As I attended more medical lectures, I became much more confident and soon I was enjoying general nursing as much as I had the psychiatric training.

Another of our lecturers at that time was a distinguished Jewish professor. When he was taking groups of students round the ward, if any of them could not answer his questions after examining the patient, I was expected to know the answer – and I usually did! This same professor had a particular interest in jaundice. He always told his students that this was not a disease on its own, but a symptom of something else. Sadly he died comparatively young, and jaundice was a prominent symptom of his illness.

The famous McKay Hart of Glasgow gave lectures in Obstetrics. He was a wonderful lecturer and had the

McKay Hart
Consultant Obstetrician
My tutor in Glasgow and colleague in Nairobi

gift of making his subject sound simple. Unlike some professors, he never forgot the human angle, and he would often ask us: "What would you do now if this was your sister?" I remember one occasion when I was in the operating theatre with him at the Eastern. The theatre sister told me to get a particular instrument, and being inexperienced I picked up the wrong one. She roared at me: "Look at that Nicolson, with the red hair showing under her cap!" But Mr. Hart reminded her: "Sister, you were young yourself once!"

HOLIDAY CONSULTATIONS

During my nursing training I always went home to Orinsay for summer holidays. In those days (1940s) my friend Sophie Kennedy and I were the only nurses for miles and all the locals, friends of Father, would drop by to ask us about their health. On one occasion when I arrived home from Glasgow Father said: "Angus Nicolson is waiting to see you. He has tablets a visiting doctor took out of his pocket and gave him. Angus didn't take them – he left them on the mantle-piece and now they've turned green!"

"Green?" I asked. "If he got those tablets for his heart they must be Digoxin – they should be green. He should never have left them lying – he should have swallowed them straight away!"

I went to see Angus and he described how he didn't trust the doctor at all. As well as handing out the green pills, he had advised Angus to walk backwards up hill to his home. This advice sounded perfectly sensible to me, but it made no sense to the patient. I explained to Angus that if he walked up the hill backwards he would find this took the weight off his heart and chest so that he would not be so breathless.

KILLEARN HOSPITAL

By 1944 I was a qualified SRN also. Before settling down to further study, I worked for a year at Killearn Hospital, in the Neurosurgical Unit. At this time there were a lot of ex-servicemen requiring treatment. This experience awakened my interest in Neurosurgery, and later led to me working with Professor Dott at Edinburgh Royal Infirmary. We had a good time in Killearn. The Saturday night dances were great fun. From my princely salary of £10.00 per month, I was able to treat myself to a new bicycle.

Later the Neurosurgical Unit moved to the Southern General in Glasgow. It makes me sad to see the old hospital building at Killearn lying derelict. I am told that buyers are not interested in it because so much asbestos was used in its construction during the War.

In those days however many courses you had completed, you were not considered a real nurse unless you had trained as a midwife. So I gritted my teeth and went back to being a junior again, training at Lennoxcastle School of Midwifery. I was encouraged that my friend May Doran was training with me, and also that the wonderful McKay Hart was in charge of the School. His unit occupied the bottom end of the Lennoxcastle site; the Castle end housed mentally deficient patients.

In fact my year at Lennoxcastle was more fun than I had expected. As well as the midwives, there were the staff from the other unit who shared the same dining room. Soon most of us young midwives had boyfriends from the hospital – nearly everyone had a click!

Cycling was very popular then and we would all ride off into the country and have a good time. But one evening I managed to break my ankle as I came off the bike. Luckily I was in the hospital grounds and not halfway up a hill. I was fortunate too that I had finished Part One of the training, but I was held back several months by this accident and did not pass Part Two until July 1948. I wanted to go home to Lewis during my convalescence, but Matron insisted that I stay at Lennoxcastle. She had me at work feeding babies in the Post Natal Ward while I was still on crutches. "If you go home now", she warned, "you will never come back to do Part Two." How right she was! I remember the same lady haranguing us about the pension scheme. In those days many girls looked forward to cashing-in their superannuation when they changed jobs, but Matron pointed out that if we waited until we retired we would get a handsome pension. Changed days! Now nobody is allowed to raid her pension fund until she is sixty, and there is no question of giving up nursing if you get married.

Training for Part Two of the Midwifery Exam required me to work as a District Trainee. Though based at Montrose Street, in the City Centre, I had to go to all the poor parts of Glasgow: Bridgeton, The Gorbals, Gallowgate, and Whiteinch. On one occasion the Sister asked me to assist her on a private nursing job, the confinement of a well-off Jewish woman. This lady had planned to have her baby in a private nursing home, but on the night she was unable to contact the establishment. Someone seemed to have left their 'phone off the hook. She called Montrose Street and soon Sister and I were on our way to Terregles Avenue. While the eminent obstetrician was enjoying a rest, the experienced midwife decided to speed things up by giving the mother a hot enema – it sounds horrid, but our patient was very pleased when it brought on her contractions. We then roused the obstetrician, who performed an episiotomy and delivered a healthy boy – to the delight of the family. The house was well-furnished and there were not one but two spotless single beds in the delivery room; the idea was that the mother would give birth in one, and then after we had cleaned her up she could roll into the other bed to sleep. The Sister earned five pounds for her efforts, and I was paid a very welcome £1.00 – a useful addition to the £6-odd I earned per month.

I also helped at a very different birth in a Bridgeton tenement. There were potatoes stored under the bed, and our patient was lying under Army greatcoats instead of blankets. Her bare feet stuck out of the covers, and the soles were pot black, because there were no carpets or linoleum on the floor. I was always amazed how obliging the people in places like that were to one another. No matter what time of the day or night it was, people would chap on a neighbour's door and ask for a loan of whatever it was they required – the most simple things such as needle and thread often had to be borrowed.

When the time came for me to sit my Midwifery exam, I was pleased to see that the Senior Consultant, Sir Hector MacLellan, was the same doctor who had supervised the birth at Terregles Avenue. He did not recognise me, but because I had worked with him I was well placed to give him the answers he wanted.

"If you were in a private house and the baby was crying, what would be wrong?" asked the Consultant.

"If the baby was crying he would be hungry," I said. "I'd give him a feed so that he wouldn't disturb the whole household – the father would be going to work in the morning and he would need his sleep." At that time – 1948 – the 'experts' believed that babies should receive their feeds at regular intervals and not before, but my answer pleased the Consultant – as I knew it would. Only after he had congratulated me on my commonsense did I reveal that I had worked with him at the private confinement. "That's why you're so good, nurse!" he commented – and I knew then I was through. "Where do you come from?" he asked. And I was proud to tell him I was from Lewis.

We were required to collect the afterbirth and take it back to the hospital for examination. One of my fellow-midwives absent-mindedly left the placenta on a bus! She had to go to the bus depot in to retrieve it – very embarrassing.

THE WAY THINGS WERE

When I had gained five Nursing certificates, I asked my father if he would help me to go to University. "Haven't you done enough?" he asked. I knew he did not have the money to pay my tuition fees and lodgings. Besides, he expected me to get married young, and if I did then any studying I had done would be wasted so far as he was concerned.

Yet several of our neighbours on Lewis had succeeded in putting their sons through University. One family in Gravir sold cattle every autumn to pay for their lads, one a student minister, the other studying medicine, at Glasgow University. The Divinity student was the same Kenneth Nicolson who witnessed the start of the Garyvard Revival. His brother Murdo went to work in Hong Kong where he met and married an American lady. But many years later after his wife had passed away he returned to end his days in his home village of Gravir.

Even more remarkable was one of our neighbours in Havelock Lane, a widow who funded the education of her two sons by gutting herring. Both her boys became ministers of religion. They had to go to Australia to find work, though one later returned to Scotland, where his son Norman McLeod achieved distinction as Sheriff Principal.

At that time – late 1930s/1940s – those crofters' sons who had made it to University lived very much like the medieval students must have done. They literally slept on straw, in the cheapest lodgings they could find. They would arrive at the start of term with a load of food from home – oatmeal and potatoes – and try to make this last as long as possible. The half term holiday at St. Andrews University is still called 'Meal Monday' because that was the time when students used to dash home for more supplies, but the Lewismen could not afford to travel back to the Island more than once a year.

During my childhood I knew of only one lady, my primary school teacher Bellann McLeod, who had attended a mainland college. She must have had an even tougher time than the male students, because of course girls were expected to look smart. Her mother made a point of dyeing Bellann's coat every summer, so that when she returned to College her city friends would think she had a new one!

In a way I am jealous of the women of today who have as good a chance of getting an education as the men, and who don't have to choose between a career and marriage the way girls of my generation had to. Yes, I said 'girls' – I still talk about my sisters and my surviving friends as 'girls' though we are all pushing eighty. During my forty-odd years as a nurse it would have been considered very strange for a wife to go out to work while her man stayed home to mind the children, yet nowadays this is a common arrangement where the woman is capable of earning more than her husband. And it amazes me that so many families can run a car, something which was a great luxury before the War!

On the minus side, I believe that many of the so-called careers which women juggle alongside their family commitments are really boring routine jobs. My mother certainly had a hard life as a crofter's wife, but she also had a chance to use her hands and her brain in all sorts of ways. She reared sheep, carded fleeces, dyed wool, spun yarn, finished tweed, grew vegetables, dried fish, lugged seaweed from the beach – all the time minding the five of us. She was always very jolly, perhaps because she was working for herself and her family and no one else.

I myself worked long hours both as a trainee and as a qualified nurse, but I knew from the start that I had chosen the right career. Pity the poor graduate nurse who enters the ward after years at college, all theory and no practical experience.

PSYCHIATRIC NURSING IN SCOTLAND

Having successfully finished my Midwifery course, in 1948 I decided to return to my original speciality: psychiatric nursing. I was appointed Departmental Sister at Hartwood Psychiatric Hospital, where I worked closely with the Deputy Medical Superintendent, Rankine Good. At that time Rankine was still married to his first wife, and I never dreamt that our paths would cross again.

After two years at Hartwood I moved on to a private mental hospital, Craighouse in Morningside, Edinburgh where I stayed for another three busy and happy years.

Rankine Good

Anne on a camel with May Doran in the Libyan desert en route to Uganda

UGANDA

At this time my good friends John and Shona Gillon were working in Kampala, the capital of Uganda. I had promised to visit them, and they were only too glad to entertain me and my pal May Doran. Originally I had hoped to persuade the Colonial Office to pay my fare to East Africa, but the only contract they would offer me was as a teacher of Psychiatry in Hong Kong. This did not fit in with my plans, so May and I set off to Uganda at our own expense – the fare to Entebbe was £92 each. On our way we enjoyed a stop-over in Libya, hence the picture of me aboard a camel. It was my first experience of Africa.

The Gillons met us at Entebbe Airport. I was anxious to start work right away, because I had spent all my savings on the fare and tropical gear, but John and Shona talked us into enjoying an eight week holiday with them before we looked for work. We had visited Lake Victoria, where the famous movie *African Queen* was filmed. I remember looking at what I thought was a rocky beach like one on Lewis. Then the Captain threw a stone and I discovered that most of the 'rocks' were huge crocodiles. We disembarked at a safer spot and walked up to the top of the Murchiston Falls from where we had a wonderful view over the Lake.

Our host John Gillon was an accountant, and he kindly invited us to join him on a trip to the Belgian Congo where he had to conduct an audit. As we drove up to the Mine we heard the native drums announcing our visit. The servants immediately set to making us a meal. There was no doubt the meat was fresh – I saw the poor chicken beheaded as we arrived!

On our return to Uganda, we had to break our

John Gillon (in highland dress)
The accountant who stood guarantor for Anne and May Doran
(Uganda 1950's)

journey at a primitive motel – a wooden hut which cost us one shilling per night each.

When we were living in Kampala, John would take Shona and the two of us with him every Saturday night for a dance and a few drinks. There were a lot of jokes about John and his harem – he had three white girls when most men had none. It wasn't long before May and I had boyfriends of our own, who helped us enjoy our stay in Uganda.

When our eight weeks holiday was over, both May and I started work at the Kampala Hospital. We would have preferred to go to the African Teaching Hospital at Mulago, but at the time we had no choice. Kampala Hospital catered almost exclusively for white patients, though there were many African staff. One night I came across John, one of the Ugandan orderlies sleeping on duty. I told him off but I didn't report him to the Matron. He showed his appreciation by teaching me some Luganda, the local language. "When I say, 'What is your tribe?' you say 'Scotch'" said John. I raised my eyebrows and explained "we don't use the word 'tribe'." But John put me right, saying: "I know the Scotch are very proud – they are the biggest tribe in England!"

Failure to get into the African Teaching Hospital and second-rate pay persuaded May Doran and me to return to the UK after only a year abroad. We immediately went to the Colonial Office to obtain new jobs in Africa – on better pay, this time! The Office wanted to send me back to Uganda, but I preferred to take a short contract in Kenya with the promise of a good gratuity at the end of two years. May and I both found posts in Kenya, but she was sent to work as a Health Visitor in Kagamega, away up-country, whilst I was assigned to the King George VI Hospital (now the Kenyatta) in Nairobi.

KENYA

In spite of all my UK training and the year I had spent working in Kampala, I was very ignorant about tropical diseases. When I found myself in charge of two wards of the King George VI Hospital and a veranda full of TB patients, I realised just how much I had to learn. Of course I had seen plenty of tuberculosis sufferers in Scotland, but I had never seen patients coughing up cupfuls of blood from their ruined lungs. To begin with, in 1956, we could not get the streptomyacin which was saving lives in the West.

We had only very limited supplies of antibiotics which were meant to be kept for the most severe cases.

One of my two wards was full of sick babies, accompanied by their mothers who were often in a worst state than the wee ones. The second ward was divided in two. One half was for sick women, the other for older children suffering from protein deficiency – kwashiorkor. Often the children's hearts were enlarged as a result of this condition. The experts said these youngsters should be started on small meals so as not to strain their hearts, but I soon discovered that they thrived much better if they got big platefuls from the beginning. I have never been afraid to trust my first-hand experience if it contradicts medical orthodoxy.

All the patients, no matter what the reason for their admission, had parasites. These were far more troublesome than the threadworms which I had encountered in Scotland. I had to learn to deal with roundworms – horrid eel-like beasts the length of your finger. Many patients were diagnosed as having appendicitis, but when the surgeons operated, roundworms were found to have caused the symptoms. One of the women in my ward was very ill, but she had no temperature and I knew she was not suffering from pneumonia, though she had a slight cough. I called the Indian doctor and described her symptoms. He began to examine her, and at that moment she coughed and ejected a huge roundworm that had been stuck in her windpipe.

Tapeworms were also very common. At the beginning of my nursing training, duties included checking the patients' stools for sections of tapeworm they had passed. So long as the head remained attached to the patient's gut, the worm could grow a new body. Thank goodness it has been discovered that one of the medicines prescribed to treat malaria has the side-effect of killing tapeworms. A small dose of this drug is enough to detach the tapeworm, and then the patient is able to void the worm, head and all, in one piece – perhaps as long as two metres! To everyone's amusement, the poisoned tapeworms are bright yellow instead of their usual dull colour.

Another parasite which is easily controlled by modern medicine is the insect which causes bilharzia. Now the illness can be cured in nine days! Many of my Kenyan patients belonged to the Luo tribe who made their living fishing in Lake Victoria. The insect would burrow under their skin while they were working. I used to wonder how Humphrey Bogart and Katherine Hepburn had escaped infection when they were filming on the Lake.

Ticks are really animal parasites rather than human ones, but people can and do become very ill as a result of tick fever, spread by the bites of these insects.

If I didn't know much about tropical diseases when I arrived in Nairobi, I soon learnt. Many of the Kenyan orderlies were very knowledgeable. Some of them had worked in prison camps during the uprising in Kenya.

I had been puzzling over the diagnosis of a very sick baby who had been brought to the hospital. I thought perhaps he had meningitis of the brain. As soon as the orderly heard that the wee soul was nine days old, he correctly guessed 'tetanus'. The incubation period for tetanus is nine days. This baby had been condemned to death by the well-meaning neighbour who cut his cord with a dirty razorblade. There was nothing we could do to save him.

While working in Kenya I made a big effort to learn some Swahili, so that I could communicate directly with the patients, instead of needing an orderly to translate everything. Each night I would write up a list of words I wanted to learn and stick it on the back of the door. I am proud to say that I passed my exam at the first attempt and qualified for a bonus as a Swahili speaker.

My responsibilities at the hospital included a twice weekly tour of every ward. I would go round in the evening when most of the European staff had gone home. Thanks to my Swahili studies I was able to make some small talk: "How's your knee?" "Did you sleep well?" in the patients' own language.

Many children would be brought into Children's Ward at night, desperately ill, wrapped in bath towels or any other cloth the parents could find. I would go round with a basket of medicines, while the doctor was examining the patients and Fr. White was giving the Last Rites. "Father White," I said to him after one awful evening of screaming children, "surely we'll get to Heaven after all this!"

"If we don't, lassie, we're damned fools in this life!" he quipped. Fr. White had been in Kenya for over thirty years, since before I was born.

A NEW CHALLENGE : SCHOOL OF MIDWIFERY

At that time the three ethnic groups: Africans, Indians and Europeans each had their own hospitals with nurses of their own but because of a serious staff shortage the Director of Medical Services asked me to take over the Indian Maternity Hospital in Nairobi for a

The team at the Lady Grigg Indian Maternity Hospital, Nairobi.
Anne and assistant midwives (late 1950's)

weekend. Though the hospital was a training centre for Assistant Midwives, I reckoned there was a great deal wrong with the set-up and I at once got busy putting things right. I made such a good impression that the Director asked me to stay on as Matron, at a larger salary than I was earning at the King George VI. He said he would make sure that I would not lose the gratuity attached to my King George VI contract. The new job was a tremendous challenge, which I accepted.

When I took charge of the Lady Grigg Indian Maternity Hospital, I was surprised to find there were several babies and young children who had been left there when their parents went off to India. This sort of thing would never have happened in a British maternity unit. Apart from the fact that the hospital was not a good place to bring up a baby, the children themselves could become a threat to the well-being of the new-borns. I found one of the resident Indian children swathed in bandages. He was suffering from pemphigus, a highly infectious disease which could easily have spread to the mothers and babies. Before I could have him transferred to a children's ward elsewhere, the poor wee lad died. I was required to attend Court – for the first and last time in my life. I explained that this practice of leaving young children in a maternity hospital would never be tolerated in the UK. Even if a baby had no family to claim him, he would be moved from the maternity unit to somewhere more suitable. The Court accepted my explanation.

To my horror I discovered that the Maternity Hospital's autoclave was not working properly, and so there was a risk of infection from instruments that had not been thoroughly sterilised. I immediately had it repaired. Any money for repairs such as this had to be

Foundation of new Nurses Home at the Indian Maternity. The Head of The Social Services League who founded the Hospital with Lady Bearing and Parsee Byramjee

obtained from the Social Service League, which was headed by a Mr. Byramjee, a rich Parsee. As well as preparing a well-argued case for each fund application, I used psychology. If one of the League members was a keen gardener, I would chat to him about plants. Perhaps another person had a special interest in the care of premature infants – I would give him the latest news of the Premature Infant Unit.

When I became Matron, I had to sleep upstairs in the hospital. I could not help hearing the noise as visitors to the nurses came and went at all hours. The most senior nurse had been in training for only ten months. If there was a difficult case, I would get up and attend to her myself.

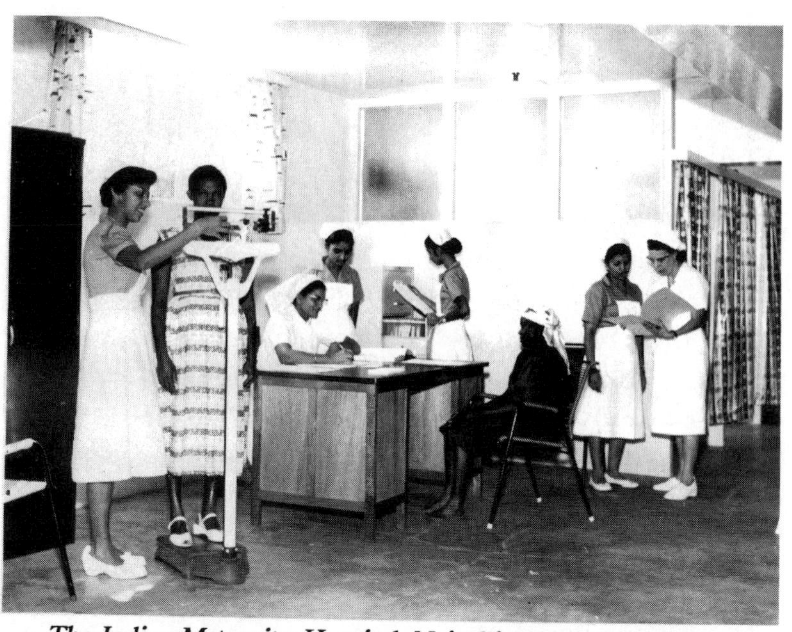

The Indian Maternity Hospital, Nairobi c1960. A basement converted into a clinic

When I took over at the Maternity Hospital, patients would often accept food brought to their window by friends. This led to gravy stains down the curtains and other mess. There is an Indian tradition that after giving birth the mother should eat a special meal, and naturally I did not interfere with this custom. But I did ask the patients if afterwards they would restrict themselves to food prepared in the hospital. I hired trained cooks and instructed them to prepare several different menus every day, suitable for the various groups of patients, Muslims and Hindus. I used to visit the kitchens first thing in the morning to see that all was well and to discuss the breakfast menu.

The first holiday that I took in Scotland after

being appointed Matron, I recruited a Midwife Tutor in Edinburgh who was willing to come to Kenya and take over the teaching. A smart new uniform was introduced for the staff. Money was found to build a new Nurses' Home, where every student had her own room. I myself had a flat on the ground floor, complete with a servant – for whom I had to pay!

It was only after I had been in charge of the Maternity Hospital for a couple of years that I was allowed to break with tradition and admit African and European mothers, as well as Indians. Later still I introduced the first African student of Midwifery, despite a lot of resistance, and towards the end of my stay a few Europeans began training there too.

In the comparatively short time I was in charge of the Lady Grigg the standard of hygiene improved so

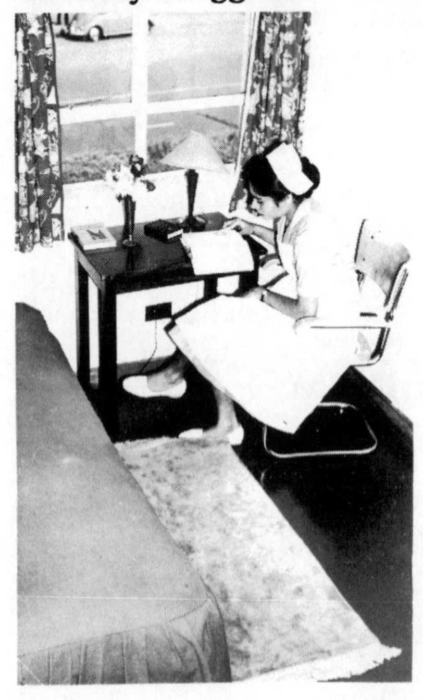

Study/bedroom in the home for trainee midwives. Anne campaigned for these facilities

much that a Sikh lady who would have normally gone to a private hospital chose to have her baby under my care. The baby, Mira, weighed only two and a half pounds when she was born and she had a rough time. The family's own doctor actually pronounced her dead, but I refused to accept this. Placing the wee girl in a cot beside her mother, I turned to one of the student midwives, a young woman called Balbir Singh, and told her: "If that baby dies, you're for it!" She nursed the baby so well that there was an immediate improvement. The father, Jaswant Singh (of whom more later) was so delighted with the way I had cared for his daughter that he insisted I become Mira's god-mother. I am still in touch with her forty years on.

I made sure that our students received a thorough training, but to begin with they could only qualify as Assistant Midwives. I was determined to raise the standards. By that time I was on the General Nursing Council of Kenya, and I set my sights on upgrading the hospital to produce fully qualified midwives whose qualifications would be recognised in the UK and elsewhere. It was a hard struggle, and a lot of people put obstacles in my way, but I succeeded in the end.

There were so many changes necessary if the School of Midwifery was to be upgraded. For instance, every book in our library had to be approved. I determined to bring my old tutor, Mr. McKay Hart, out to Nairobi. He was on the Board of the Royal College of Midwives in Edinburgh and he had to obtain their permission before he could come to Kenya to organise the medical hierarchy in the hospital. There was also the little matter of finding the money to pay for his visit. We had a Punch & Judy show in the hospital compound to raise the money, and in due course

During the visit of McKay Hart and his wife.
Deputy Matron Savitri Gulame and Anne

Mr. Hart and his wife came to Kenya. I was delighted to put them up in my house. We welcomed the Harts with a party in the hospital grounds. There was a big spread of vegetarian dishes on one side and an equally lavish selection of meat curries on the other, plus loads of sweets. In fact, there were so many parties during his visit that Mr. Hart remarked to me that he had not seen his pyjamas since he arrived! Maybe this was how he came to leave them behind when he returned to Scotland.

During McKay Hart's stay, he was asked to operate on a patient. I remember him saying to me as we approached the theatre: "I hope I do this OK!" It was a revelation to me that such a distinguished obstetrician should be nervous.

One of Mr. Hart's quirks was that he refused to wear gloves when examining patients. Even in those pre-AIDS days this was considered dangerous for the doctor, but McKay Hart did not care. He claimed he could diagnose symptoms better with his bare hands.

Perhaps because we had looked after Mr. Hart so well, Professor Donald of the Queen Mother's Maternity Hospital in Glasgow began to send doctors to Kenya to help with training.

The Harts' stay in Kenya coincided with Mrs. Ghandi's visit to the Maternity Hospital, and they joined me in entertaining her in my house. Indira Ghandi, was then the Indian Foreign Secretary. As you can imagine, her visit attracted tremendous interest amongst Kenyan Indians, who regarded Nehru's daughter almost as a goddess. However, many of the

Mrs Indira Ghandi, Indian Foreign Minister, being shown round the hospital by Anne

local Indians were shocked when they learnt that Mrs. Ghandi had taken a glass of wine when she was dining in a Nairobi hotel. To make matters worse, not only had Mrs. Ghandi taken alcohol, but the wine was from South Africa, which at that time operated the notorious apartheid policy! That wine, 'La Gratitude', was actually banned in Kenya from then on. I made a point of trying it when I was next in Britain, and I found it delicious – Mrs. Ghandi had good taste.

Glad though I was to meet Mrs. Ghandi, I was even more interested to meet Margaret Myles, the author of the famous midwifery textbook. I was very proud when she later wrote to my parents saying how impressed she had been by the way I ran the Lady Grigg Hospital.

Treetops Hotel
Kenya

Margaret Myles and I visited the Treetops Hotel – the place where Princess Elizabeth had been staying when she learnt of the death of King George, her father. At the time of our visit, Treetops was still very small, accommodating only half a dozen guests. When we arrived, a guide took us up the path through a welcoming committee of elephants! As we climbed the steps into the hotel, a gang of monkeys descended on us looking for titbits. When we took tea and biscuits in the lounge, most of the biscuits were stolen. Luckily the monkeys retired early, and we were able to relax and enjoy the spectacle of the wild animals visiting the water hole and licking the salt left out for them. The next day we visited nearby towns such as Nyeri before returning to Nairobi.

I would have been quite content for the Government to take over the Lady Grigg Hospital as the central midwifery training college for Kenya, but the Indians who owned the Hospital refused. I think some of them had plans for a private hospital which would make money! When the Government wanted to transfer me to another hospital, I did not object. I was ready for a new challenge.

KIAMBU GENERAL HOSPITAL

Kiambu was a large general hospital some ten miles from Nairobi. It had a big midwifery unit attached. Besides running Kiambu, I was responsible for patients in the sickbay at the nearby prison, Kamiti, and I had to visit a small general hospital five or six miles away in the heart of coffee plantations. One of the staff at the small hospital was a man called Joseph Munuhe with whom I had worked before. He was a very capable nurse and ran the hospital efficiently.

The biggest problem facing me at Kiambu was the number of patients needing treatment. Rather than leave sick people to die in the hospital grounds, leaning against a tree, I preferred to admit them even if this meant two or three patients sharing a bed overnight.

This may shock you, but is it any worse than leaving someone on a trolley in the hospital corridor for hours and hours? Often the next day a patient would be fit enough to go home, and the newcomer would have the bed to himself.

In those days – late 1950s – judicial hangings still took place in Kenya. When a prisoner was due to be executed, the atmosphere in the whole prison became very sombre. I myself had no contact with the condemned men, but I know that the local Roman Catholic priest would visit them on death row and do all he could to make their last days bearable. He would smuggle in whisky or other wee luxuries to help pass their last night. I am glad to say that after Independence the death penalty was abolished in Kenya.

I was able to make a small contribution to the welfare of the prisoners who were kept in an open ward in the grounds of the main sickbay. I often visited this group late at night, after 10pm when the rest of the hospital was asleep. I would bring sweeties and newspapers for the prisoners, and a few sleeping pills. I knew that if I left these drugs with the staff the prisoners would never get any, so I made sure that the men who needed sleeping pills swallowed them immediately.

I decided that the hospital grounds needed a good clean-up, and I recruited a squad of prisoners from Kamiti to do the job – which was not an easy one. Though there was a hospital cemetery where unclaimed bodies were buried, funeral arrangements for these patients left a lot to be desired. Graves were not dug deep enough, with the result that stray dogs would disturb them and scatter human remains. I determined to put an end to this disgrace, but the solution did not come in the way that I would have expected. The Scots Minister from Nairobi began to visit the main hospital regularly, and I would invite staff to join us if they could. The man responsible for burying the paupers was one of the staff members who became Christian. I noticed that after his conversion he managed the cemetery much better.

Many of the hospital staff were already Christians, mostly the products of Scottish Missions up-country. Many of these Africans believed that it was a sin to smoke tobacco, and they would have been horrified to see the Scots Minister enjoying a cigarette at my house when he was off-duty. "This is my holy smoke," he quipped.

Because of the shortage of qualified doctors, we relied very heavily on medical assistants, many of whom had trained in the camps during the Emergency. They used to deal with huge outpatient clinics, and they were excellent at deciding who needed to be admitted to the hospital wards. On one occasion they had six people admitted, who were suffering the after-effects of eating carrion. This was unusual; Kikuyu Kenyans are as fussy about eating fresh meat as we Scots. The medical students referred to their textbooks and decided that these patients should all be dead. Thankfully the books were wrong on this occasion and all six recovered. When they were feeling better, I asked one of them which bit of the fallen cow she had eaten. "The sweetbreads!" she admitted, laughing at herself.

Some of the medical assistants supplemented their income by giving private treatment after hours. If you have ever had toothache, you will understand why some desperate people would pay an assistant to remove a rotten tooth by tying a ligature round the tooth, looping the string over his foot and pulling hard. But you may be surprised to learn that the medical assistants also did a good line in cosmetic surgery. Many Kenyan women in those days had spoiled their ear lobes by wearing earrings that were far too heavy. The assistants would skilfully trim the lobes, and send the ladies home looking much prettier.

I am amused to read that it is now considered very progressive to give nurses in the UK responsibility to treat minor ailments. Those Kenyan assistants were years ahead of their time!

The Kaimbu hospital was modern in another respect too. Its operating theatre was used intensively. In addition to the routine operations performed during the day, it was used at night for emergencies. Dr. Beecher, a missionary doctor whose father was Bishop of Mombasa, lived in the hospital grounds. He was easy to contact, and he was most obliging in giving emergency treatment. Because he had been brought up in East Africa, Dr. Beecher was fluent in both Kikuyu and Swahili, the principal local languages. Though the operating theatre itself was spotless, the disposal of surgical material was unsatisfactory – the doctors would drop the debris out of the window into a pail, from where it was promptly grabbed by a stray dog!

Now at the beginning of my stay in Kaimbu, one of my Scottish friends, Janet Love, the former Matron of Motherwell Maternity Hospital, came to Kenya on a visit. I asked her to take on the maternity unit for a short time, for a token salary. Miss Love ran into problems with tribal traditions.

On the whole the Kikuyu nursing staff were excellent, but their tribe had a taboo against cleaning lavatories, etc. For example, my house servant offered to do all sorts of extra jobs for me if I would only clean the toilet myself. I was happy to come and go with him, and we got on fine. However in the hospital itself things were more difficult. Normally a maternity nurse would be expected to give patients bedpans as required, and to clean the pans afterwards. The Kikuyu nurses would hand out the bedpans readily enough, but they wanted to leave the cleaning to the 'sweepers', who all belonged to a another tribe with different customs. When Miss Love insisted that the midwives should clean the bedpans themselves, there was nearly a strike. But my friend stood firm, and told the Kikuyu staff that if they did withdraw their labour they would be dismissed.

In my early days at Kaimbu, I set about improving the standard of hospital food. The kitchens were very primitive, and often the staple maize porridge "uji" would arrive in the ward only half cooked. I could sympathise with the kitchen staff, who had to struggle into work on bicycles over muddy roads during the Rains, and then attempt to get the boilers going. But human rights begin with breakfast, and so they were strictly forbidden to send out food that was not properly cooked. I reckoned it would be better for patients to wait for their breakfast than to get a bowlful of food they could not digest. If there were any doubts about the edibility of the porridge, the patients would keep a sample for me to adjudicate on later!

Having set the standard for breakfast, I tackled the problem of lunch. By midday the boilers were burning nicely, and there was no technical reason why the patients should not have enjoyed a hot meal with meat and vegetables. I suspected that a lot of the hospital meat was walking out through the gate. I began random searches of kitchen staff, and they soon realised that they would have to start buying their own supplies. The quality of hospital meals at Kaimbu improved out of all recognition, and the patients benefited from a healthy diet.

During my time at Kaimbu, I received a complaint from the local general store that the smell from the hospital mortuary was driving away their customers. I investigated and was upset to find that the stretcher bearers were in the habit of dumping dead bodies on the floor and on top of one another. Even the doctors who performed post mortem examinations in the mortuary were very careless in a way that would not be tolerated in Britain. The root of the problem seemed to be another of those Kikuyu taboos – they refused to handle corpses just as they would not clean up excreta.

I called a staff meeting and announced that from then on if a patient died, his or her body was to be escorted to the morgue by a member of the nursing staff and decently laid out by itself. I also made sure we employed 'sweepers' from non-Kikuyu tribes who would keep the mortuary clean. Later on I had to scotch a racket run by a hospital telephone operator who told next of kin that they could not remove their dead from the mortuary until they had paid him a tip. Not only did he rob the relatives, but he created a backlog of unclaimed bodies. Only by taking a personal interest in this unglamorous part of the hospital did I put things right. I used to inspect the morgue each morning.

INDEPENDENCE

When I came to Kenya in 1956 the Kikuyu leader Jomo Kenyatta was still in custody. He had been released from prison but he was required to stay in Githunguri. While he was living there, he got in touch with the lawyer who had defended him, Jaswant Singh, and asked him to come to visit him and to bring his family. One of Jaswant's daughters was Mira, my god-daughter who had been born in the Lady Grigg Indian Maternity.

Through my friendship with the Singh family, later I had the opportunity to meet Jomo Kenyatta and his sister Margaret in Jaswant's house. I was very impressed by the Kikuyu leader, though many of my fellow Europeans regarded him as a terrorist. As a young man Kenyatta had studied at Woodbrooke, the Quaker college near Birmingham. There he formed his philosophy: *"We, the children of humanity, being brothers and sisters, must serve one another in the love of all mankind. This spirit, I hold, must rule and pervade all classes of the community irrespective of rank or station, colour or race."* What took forty words to say in English could be condensed into one Swahili word "Harambee" – the motto of Kenya!

Years later when he was president of an independent Kenya, he made a practice of broadcasting at 11am every day. Most of his broadcasts were very sensible, but one day he rashly announced that the charge of one Kenyan shilling imposed on people attending outpatient clinics was to be abolished, and all prescriptions would be dispensed free of charge. There was a near-riot at Kaimbu, and we had to call the

Jomo Keynatta
Father of the Nation

police to keep order with clubs! I was reminded of the early days of the NHS in Scotland, when some people used the cottonwool they had been given as dusters. Of course, everyone wants something for nothing. I would say that the Kenyan shilling that the outpatients used to pay was perhaps equivalent to £5.00 in Britain in 2002. I was surprised to see one women attend the hospital that day who had nearly lost a finger because her ring was too tight. She must have been in terrible pain, and yet she had been put off seeking treatment because of the one shilling levy.

Shortly after my audience with Kenyatta, another Goan lawyer who had previously defended him was murdered. Jaswant was afraid that Kenyatta's enemies would come after him too, and so he cleared out to England, taking his wife, Mira and the rest of his family with him. Later he left the family in London and worked overseas, but he was never allowed to set foot in Kenya again.

As well as being a brilliant advocate, Jaswant was a wonderful speaker in private life. I could listen to him for hours. He told some fascinating stories about his triumphs in court, how he would manage to get a client off through his knowledge of the law.

When Independence came in 1962, the so-called Freedom Fighters were released from prison. Some of them applied to Kaimbu Hospital for work. Sadly I found that many of these men had not benefited from their time behind bars the way the Camp-trained medical assistants had. Many of these ex-prisoners would have caused trouble in any society.

In Kaimbu an African Kenyan took over as Medical Officer of Health. Every morning there was a long queue of people waiting to see him. Some of these were staff who were to be disciplined for some fault, others looked suspiciously like high-class call girls.

However, it was for personal reasons rather than political ones that I finally decided to leave Kenya. I was engaged to be married. My fiancé and I had got as far as ordering our cake. Then something happened which made me realise that the marriage would never succeed. I ended the engagement and decided that the best thing for me to do would be to leave Kenya and return to Scotland to be near my elderly parents. So in 1966 I came home.

SCOTLAND IN THE 1960s

The first thing I did on my return from Kenya was to travel to Orinsay to spend some time with my Mother and Father, who by this time were both over eighty years of age.

Next I took a temporary job at Stobhill Maternity Unit in Glasgow, before joining the staff of the new Queen Mother's Hospital at Yorkhill. The facilities were excellent but the pay poor, and so I soon left for a post in Psychiatric Nursing at Gartnavel. It was while I was working at Gartnavel that Rankine Good, my old colleague from Hartwood, learnt that I was back in town – and still unmarried. By this time Rankine had been divorced for about three years. He came up to the Hospital where I was working, and asked to see me. From then on things moved swiftly. I had no doubts about my feelings for Rankine, but I must admit that I was reluctant to leave my flat in the West End of Glasgow for Motherwell where he lived. Rankine's house on Hamilton Road was lovely, but the steel town of Motherwell was not very attractive in itself.

We married in 1971, and all Rankine's three daughters came along to wish us well. Though my new husband did not share my enthusiasm for entertaining at home, he had many other interests outside his profession. He loved learning languages, and was fluent in seven – speaking as well as reading. Because I was a Gaelic speaker, he was inspired to learn that too. While he attended a beginners class I went off to classes in painting where I tried to record some of the wonderful sights I had seen in Africa. Rankine made excellent progress in Gaelic – I am sure he would have passed

Together at last.
Rankine and Anne Good shortly after their wedding

Anne's three step-daughters

the 'O' Level easily – but he was such a perfectionist that he did not think he was ready to sit the exam. Together we went to ceilidhs and concerts of traditional Highland music.

It was about this time that I saw an advertisement for a course in Meditation. I mentioned it to Rankine, and he said: "If it's about relaxation, you're needing to go!" Go I did, and within a few weeks I was benefiting from twenty minute meditations, morning and evening. I found that these sessions made me calmer and better able to cope with the stresses of the hospital.

After my marriage I accepted a post in Hartwood Hospital where Rankine was Deputy Medical Superintendent. I was in the School of Nursing. Two or three times a week I would take my class to the wards to teach them simple practical nursing. I feel sorry for the nurses of today who seem to be taught only the theory of nursing, and who are left to find out the practicalities for themselves – if they can.

Rankine was a very far-seeing man, and he anticipated the problems that would arise if experienced nurses were promoted out of the ward, as envisaged by the Salmon Committee. He suggested that it would be much better to boost their salaries, while keeping them on the front line of patient care. Meanwhile I myself left my post in the School of Nursing for the better-paid post of Assistant Matron at Hartwood.

A man of principle, Rankine was very concerned about justice, and he was not afraid to disagree with Health Board policy. At that time – early 1970s – brain operations such as leucotomies were regularly performed on mental patients. Rankine strongly opposed these treatments, which damaged the patients' brain and in his opinion did them no good at all. However he was convinced – as I am – of the value of electro-convulsive therapy (ECT) in treating depression. Many people consider this is a cruel treatment with nasty side-effects such as loss of memory, but Rankine believed that it had its uses in dealing with the most stubborn kinds of depressive illness which make life unbearable for the patient and often leads to suicide. This conclusion was not based on a snap judgement. Rankine Good took detailed notes of what his patients told him, and he supplemented these records with his observations of any next of kin who visited his patients. Behind his friendly exterior he was absolutely dedicated to his work, and he believed it was his duty to keep very detailed records of the mental patients in his care in case his opinion might be sought in legal proceedings. When he died I had to dispose of seven big sacks of shorthand notes relating to his patients.

It was about this time that the movement gathered

strength to close all the big Victorian psychiatric hospitals and place mental patients in the community. Rankine did not believe that this policy would work, and I think the last thirty years have proved him right. In the best old-style mental hospitals, such as Hartwood, staff really did try to give long-stay patients a comfortable life. Not only were they sheltered, clothed and fed, but they were encouraged to work if they could, and to enjoy activities such as dancing and music. For many people with intractable mental problems, 'care in the community' just means the freedom to be hungry, cold, dirty and lonely.

Rankine decided to retire rather than wait to see all the work he had done at Hartwood over the years dismantled. Besides, he was not in very good health,

Anne and Rankine enjoying a holiday

Happy days with Rankine at the Golden Mosque in Jerusalem

having suffered a mild coronary.

After a short time I retired too, so that we could spend more time together. We enjoyed some super holidays together, including a visit to Jerusalem where we followed the Stations of the Cross. We would have loved to go back to the Holy City. Just before he died, Rankine was talking about returning there.

My mother Christina Nicolson, was failing at this time. Rankine accompanied me to Orinsay, where I nursed Mother for the last few days of her life. I was so glad that I was able to be there with her at the end. As her son-in-law, Rankine took an active part in the funeral, and helped to carry the coffin from our croft to the cemetery. The tradition on these occasions is that the family act as bearers for the first few hundred metres, and then all the able-bodied men in the community take their turn. People who are not good with words can show their respect for the deceased and their sympathy for the family by helping to carry the coffin. It is a very moving sight.

A year after Mother's death Rankine himself died of a massive coronary. My only consolation was that I was with him at the time and he passed away quickly, without a long painful struggle.

It goes without saying that his death was a tremendous blow to me. Our friend Dr. Markose, was devastated too; Rankine had met this young Kerelan when he was appointed Registrar at Hartwood. The two men got on very well and Rankine encouraged Dr. Markose to sit Part One of his Royal College of Medicine exam. Later I was able to help Dr. Markose with an introduction to a consultant at a hospital in Dorking. The upshot was that Dr. Markose was taken on as a Registrar, and things worked out so well that he stayed at Dorking until his retirement. Helping him took my mind off my own troubles, and in return he has looked after me as if I were his aunt.

ALLERGIES & DOWSING

I did not become interested in dowsing until 1977, after the death of my husband Rankine. As you can imagine, I had a lot of time on my hands and I was desperate to keep busy. Rankine and I had had only six years together. Once again I found myself alone in the world.

As I said before, I have had a special interest in schizophrenia since childhood, when the local lad was

Gwen Hemmings, founder of the Schizophrenia Association of Great Britian with Anne

carted off to Inverness Asylum. I decided to write to Mrs. Hemmings, founder of the Schizophrenia Association of Great Britain (SAGB) to see if I could help. She kindly invited me to a conference in England, where I heard some very interesting speakers, and where I met Professor Cyril Wilson. He was a highly qualified pharmacologist, who had left Ireland so that his wife could pursue a career in family planning. He soon found work in charge of the geriatric wards at Law Hospital, not far from Motherwell where I was living. We saw a lot of each other after the Conference. I am forever in his debt because he introduced me to the work of Amelia Nathan Hill.

Right from the start of my nursing career, I believed there was a strong connection between food and mental illness. Having studied carefully the diet of the patients in Leverndale, I came to the conclusion that mostly they were better fed at home, yet the better diet had not prevented them falling ill in the first place. Having dismissed general nutrition as a factor, I explored the possibility that vitamin deficiencies might be significant. It was only years later after I returned to Scotland from Africa that I realised that allergies – including food allergies – might be a major cause of ill health. For example, there was the English GP Richard Markarness, who was below par for years. His medical colleagues, finding him lying on his couch before a clinic, would tell him. "Get up! It's all in your mind, Richard!"

On hearing that an American physician was testing patients for sensitivity to various foods, Dr. Markarness travelled to the USA for a consultation. He was told that he had only one allergy – to coffee. As soon as he eliminated this from his diet his health improved dramatically. He applied the same principles to his own patients back in the UK, and the success of these elimination diets in identifying food allergies led to him writing his best-seller: *"Not All in the Mind"*.

One of the first patients to benefit from Dr. Markarness's diet therapy was the Italian-born Amelia Nathan Hill. During the Second World War Amelia had risked her life to take food to partisans hiding in the mountains. She also collected gold in an attempt to ransom the Jewish community in Rome. When the Nazis reneged on the deal, Amelia had to go into hiding for several years until the end of the War.

In 1945 Amelia was fit enough to work as a translator for the Allied troops, but soon after she embarked on medical studies, she fell ill. She was bedridden for four years, and her marriage to an Italian doctor broke down under the strain. Amelia tried many different sorts of treatment, all to no avail until she met Dr. Markarness. He discovered that the war heroine suffered from multiple allergies, not only to food but also to everyday hazards such as the emissions from diesel trains. Thanks to Dr. Markarness, Amelia's health improved. She learnt to distinguish between the foods and other irritants which she had to avoid entirely, and those to which she could build up a tolerance. She was so grateful for the transformation in her own life that from then on she devoted herself to publicising the treatment. In 1978 she founded 'Action Against Allergy' in England, and in 1980 she published *"Against the Unsuspected Enemy"* describing how allergies could be responsible for all sorts of illness, not only migraines and stomach upsets.

I met Amelia Nathan Hill during the early 1980s. Together we went to see Dr. Ian Menzies, a child psychiatrist practising in Dundee. He had become interested in allergies after noting how many of the mothers who consulted him reported that their children were allergic to cow's milk. He began to test his new patients for allergies, and soon he was travelling all over Scotland lecturing on the subject. Many years later it was Dr. Menzies who suggested I should write my memoirs.

Amelia Nathan Hill helped me start the Scottish branch of Action Against Allergy. She was a wonderful woman, keen to help everyone, in spite of her own health problems which she never completely overcame. She died early in 2002, after having been crippled by osteoporosis for several years. But at least Amelia lived long enough to see general recognition of the problem of allergies.

Of course, I was – and am – particularly interested in the role allergies play in mental illness. It is more than sixty years since I saw that Lewis boy put on the boat to the asylum, but I have never forgotten him. I have been retired from nursing for more than twenty years, but I have never stopped trying to help people with mental health problems identify the allergies which make their symptoms worse. Though I believe that mental illness often runs in families, I have no doubt that sufferers can help themselves a lot by learning to recognise and avoid the foods they are sensitive to.

EASTERN THERAPY IN SOUTH LANARKSHIRE

Ageism existed in the Health Service even in the 1970s, and a lot of folk saw little point in bothering with geriatric patients. But Professor Wilson thought it was his duty to do everything he could to help his patients, even if they had only a short time to live. Unfortunately not everyone agreed with the methods he used. When he instructed the nurses not to be so quick cleaning up incontinent patients, but to leave them in contact with their faeces & urine for a short time, there was a mutiny. The staff thought he had gone crazy, and that they would all end up being fired for neglecting their duties. Yet Professor Wilson was only applying a principle of Ayurvedic medicine, such as is practised by millions of people on the subcontinent of India. He believed that contact with their own bodily wastes would desensitise these elderly patients to the many allergies which afflicted them and so improve their quality of life.

This regime had nothing whatsoever to do with the neglect of geriatric patients which we occasionally read about in under-staffed nursing homes or badly-run hospitals. It was simply a method of triggering the immune systems of these elderly people, in the same way that contact with pet animals can boost children's immune systems and reduce absences from school.

You may recall the furore in the newspapers when a visiting Indian prime minister, Morarji Deshi, cheerfully admitted to drinking a tot of his own urine every morning. When he stayed at the famous Gleneagles Hotel, a glass of his water was served to him at breakfast. Just as Scots people dose their children with vitamin drops or fish oil capsules, so many Indians give their youngsters a couple of spoonfuls of cow's urine every day. I knew a Sikh family who had followed this practice, and their children were the picture of health. Ayurvedic practitioners recommend a drop of one's own urine under the tongue as a general tonic, and Professor Wilson prescribed this to his patients at Law.

The plain people of Lanarkshire were not impressed by Professor Wilson's efforts to help the geriatrics. One of the cleaners at Law Hospital was heard to remark that if there was any question of her being told to drink urine she would be off at once, and forget about her pension. Soon the Health Board ordered him to discontinue the treatment, in case relatives of the geriatric patients sued.

Ayurvedic urine therapy never did catch on in Lanarkshire, but Professor Wilson soon built up an enthusiastic following of private patients. I had the big

Activists Against Allergies
Anne with Amelia Nathan Hill and Professor Cedric Wilson

house in Motherwell which I had shared with Rankine, and I was glad to be able to help by making my lounge available for Professor Wilson's consultations. Some private patients came from as far away as Aberdeen, and I was able to give them a bed for the night in my home.

After his retirement from Law Hospital, Professor Wilson came to believe that certain of the patients who consulted him with allergies might have other problems which were spiritual and psychiatric rather than physical. He encouraged some patients to undergo exorcism by a priest, and counselled others on the best way to consolidate multiple personalities. When he referred to 'AIEs' – alien intelligent entities – possessing a sick person, I was reminded of the way my grandmother Nicolson used to talk about a naughty child being 'full of the Devil'. As a Christian I was certainly prepared to believe in the existence of evil. However, I feared that Professor Wilson was over-confident in the way he challenged these dark forces, which I believe should be treated with the same respect as a highly contagious disease. Or as the Bible tells us:

> *"Be sober, be vigilant; because your adversary the devil . . . walks about seeking whom he may devour"* [I Peter ch5 v8]

Professor Wilson might have some unusual ideas about therapy, but he had enough commonsense to know he needed a chaperone when seeing patients. I used to sit-in on his consultations, and as a result I learnt a tremendous amount about the diagnosis and treatment of allergies.

Thirty years on I still respect the privacy of Professor Wilson's patients, so there will not be any descriptions of actual cases. However, a typical scenario would be that someone had felt unwell for a while. He would try 'over the counter remedies', then consult his own G.P., then perhaps be referred to a hospital consultant – all to no avail. Finally he would hear about Professor Wilson. Though the patient might be sceptical about some of the Professor's theories, he would willingly submit to dowsing to identify his allergy or allergies. Thereafter he would try to avoid the suspect substances in the hope of a cure.

Though I had been all too familiar with 'Maryhill heads' – the distended skulls of Glaswegians whose drinking water had been contaminated by lead – I had never dreamt that ordinary tap water from copper pipes could cause problems. But after observing Professor. Wilson's consultations I became convinced that many people do suffer from an allergy to tap water. Luckily water filters are now widely available, and it is easy to purify the water you are going to drink. Unfortunately it is not so easy to filter the water used for bathing. Professor Wilson often advised patients who suffered severely from water allergy to ration the number of showers they took, and not to wash their hair for six months. This advice was nearly as unpopular as the urine therapy. Some of the patients used to fool their families by disappearing into the bathroom and turning on the shower, while furtively cleaning themselves with a face cloth. They would rub their hair with a dry towel to remove grease. Six months of restricted washing usually succeeded in restoring the patients' skin to its natural balance, and after that they could resume moderate showering, etc.

I soon noticed that many of Professor Wilson's private patients were practically addicted to the food or substance they were allergic to. For instance, if someone had an allergy to dairy products, it was odds on that she would be a keen milk drinker.

Nothing I observed while working with Professor Wilson dissuaded me from my long-held belief that allergies are very significant in mental illnesses such as schizophrenia. I am convinced that while allergies do not cause the condition, they can make it very much worse, and so I always recommend schizophrenia sufferers to undergo an allergy test. There is no need to subject everyone to an elimination diet over several days or weeks; in my experience dowsing, either with the patient present or over a sample of his hair, can be very useful in suggesting which foods or substances he is allergic to. It is then up to the patient to try cutting out one or more of the suspected irritants, and to see if he feels any better.

Anne's sister Joan McKinnon having a laugh whilst being tested

In case you are amused at the idea of swinging a pendulum over a lock of hair, remember that hair samples are used to ascertain what drugs a person has taken over a period of months. Analysis of strands of Napoleon Bonaparte's hair has led to suspicions that he was poisoned with arsenic while imprisoned on St. Helena. In the hands of an experienced dowser, a pendulum is a good tool for identifying allergies. It is quick and cheap to use, and causes no side effects. Isn't it strange that people are quite ready to believe that a pet can tell when an epileptic is about to take a turn, or a dog can smell a hidden tumour, but they will not accept that a human being can make a diagnosis by using her God-given senses? [*The Times 27 June 2002 - Dogs have nose for cancer*]

Professor Wilson organised an examination in

dowsing, which I sat along with several others. The procedures were just like those followed during any examination in conventional medicine. There was an invigilator and a strict time limit. At the end, I told the Professor that was the worst examination I had ever sat. His comment: "then I'd like to see your best!" reassured me that I must have passed, and indeed I had.

Sadly Professor Wilson is no longer with us, but I am glad to say that I am still using what I learnt from him to help people with allergies.

My interest in allergies became all the stronger after I met Amelia Nathan Hill, the founder of Action Against Allergy. However, I found that the name of the charity seemed to discourage Scots people, so I renamed Action Against Allergy (Scotland): 'FIND', Food Intolerant Nutrient Deficiency. This title stressed the need to seek out the foods the body needed, as well as to avoid the ones which caused problems.

At the time of writing this chapter I am interested to hear that a Home Office study has found that young offenders who were treated with vitamin supplements re-offended noticeably less than the control group who were dosed with a placebo. [*The Metro, 26th June 2002*] It is no surprise to me that deficiencies in nutrition can affect people's general behaviour as well as their health!

About this time I got to know David Mellon, a fully qualified nutritionist, and a fountain of knowledge. He used to have a shop on Great Western Road, but he now lives in Rutherglen. I often refer people with allergy problems to him.

Fund Raisers F.I.N.D.

FUND RAISING

For years the Salvation Army had been famous for collecting money in public houses, and I decided I would try this approach too. As well as raising funds for the charity, I found the pub visits were great for educating the public about the problem of food allergies. I would sit down with a group of drinkers in the bar and explain how schizophrenia could be exacerbated by food intolerance. My experience as a nurse tutor came in useful, and several people congratulated me on the way I put over this difficult subject. John Buchanan and Alena McLeod helped me with the collections.

As you may have heard, many Glasgow pubs are associated with one or other of the major football teams, Celtic or Rangers, and in the 1980s there was more Roman Catholic vs Protestant bigotry than there is today, when supporters of both top teams are urged to reject this prejudice. Though I myself had no interest in football, I knew enough about the Parkhead/Ibrox rivalry to exploit it. You can be sure that when I entered the Rangers pub 'The Rosevale' in Partick I was wearing a blue scarf and a jaunty blue hat! Conversely when I targeted the 'Smiddy' a few hundred metres away, I would change into a nice green beret. Both sets of fans contributed generously, but I would say that I got more cash out of the Celts in the 'Smiddy' because about that time the Bhoys had some famous victories which put their supporters in a very good mood.

I donated a computer to the Schizophrenia Association, and I dedicated the gift as a memorial to Rankine. I was also instrumental in having a small house donated to the Association. It had been occupied by a schizophrenia sufferer who had been abandoned by his family; he was so pleased with the support he got from the Association that he left the property to SAGB in his Will.

I should say here that the Schizophrenia Association does NOT share my belief in the role of allergies in schizophrenia. Though I am still a Director I have not succeeded in persuading SAGB of the importance of checking schizophrenia sufferers for allergies before any treatment is started. Such checks would have to be done in an independent laboratory otherwise the consultants would attach no importance to the results. It would be expensive, but I believe it would be worthwhile in the long run.

Fund Raisers
Schizophrenia Research.
Anne raised a great deal of money for this cause

It is surprising that after all this time that there is no specialised allergy clinic in Scotland. If you are suffering from asthma, you are referred to an asthma clinic, if you have a skin rash, you are sent to a skin clinic, etc. For years the campaign to found a Scottish allergy clinic has been led by an Edinburgh lady, Mrs. Girling, whose son committed suicide after suffering severely from a number of allergies. This year – 2002 – I hope to join Mrs. Girling and her team in the final push to found such a clinic. Now that I am listed in *Who's Who in Scotland* I may be able to help more than I could before.

MORE ABOUT DOWSING

About the time I got to know Professor Wilson, I also met a remarkable lady, Anne Shearer, who has been in charge of the Phoenix Centre in Glasgow for many years. An early exponent of dowsing, Anne Shearer is today best known for the breathing exercises she teaches to alleviate a wide range of illnesses. I feel that I have learnt as much from Anne as I did from Professor Wilson.

For many people the word 'dowsing' conjures up a picture of someone searching for underground water using a forked twig. This technique has been used since prehistoric times, to locate not only water but also minerals. There are cave paintings thousands of years old which show dowsers at work. More recently, in the 16th century, German miners came to Cornwall and dowsed for the lost tin mines, and the practice became widespread, despite the fact that it was an offence under the Witchcraft Act. In the 19th century there was renewed interest in dowsing, both in Britain and America. However it was a Frenchman, Abbé Mermet, who popularised diagnostic dowsing. He himself believed that he could detect a change in the energy fields produced by the people he examined.

During the Vietnam War, the US Marine Corps found dowsing useful in locating the enemy's underground tunnels, buried communication lines and mines. The technique can also be used to trace missing persons.

The beauty of dowsing is that most people who are interested in the subject can learn the techniques quickly and thereafter practise them in their own homes. I always tell my students that the first thing they must do is to learn their Yes and No. I ask them if there is any food or drink they are particularly keen on. Supposing they say they love milk, I immediately suspect that they are allergic to dairy products. I put the patient's hand flat on the table and place a jug of milk nearby. Then I take my own pendulum, a piece of crystal on a fine chain, and hold it about ten centimetres over the person's hand. I simply ask if the patient is allergic to milk, and if the answer is 'yes', the crystal turns clockwise. However, if there is no harm in the patient taking milk products, my crystal will swing diagonally.

Next I give the patient a pendulum of his own, and ask him to repeat the question. Some people find that for them, a positive answer is indicated by the pendulum swinging from left to right, others find that their 'yes' is a turn anti-clockwise. The next step is to rephrase the question so that the correct answer (for that particular patient) is 'no'. The crystal will once again move in a distinctive way, showing the student dowser that this is his negative. Some talented folk catch on very quickly, but it may take up to an hour to convince sceptics that this simple tool, a suspended crystal or piece of wood, can give consistent replies.

Just as some people are colour blind or tone deaf, so a tiny minority cannot learn to dowse. It is not just a matter of being sceptical, because in my experience most folk who try the technique are quickly convinced that it works independently, that is to say it is not controlled by the dowser.

Though I am chiefly interested in dowsing as a diagnostic technique, I do find it useful in other ways. For instance, if I have mislaid something at home I may use the pendulum to discover which room it is in. I suppose you could argue that this is just a way of tapping my sub-conscious memory of where I last saw the lost item – but it is quicker than waiting until bedtime and receiving the answer in a dream! Sometimes, like Luke Reinhart consulting his dice in the cult novel 'Diceman' I ask the pendulum what course of action I should follow. But unlike the reckless Diceman who found himself in all sorts of trouble, I never forget my Christian principles when framing the question!

Anyone interested in learning more about dowsing can contact the Scottish Dowsing Association c/o Good, 59 Barrington Drive, Glasgow. G4 9ES, or c/o Harper, 14 Scott Drive, Largs. KA30 9PA

THE NICEST COMPLIMENT I WAS EVER PAID

I seem to have the knack not only of making friends but of holding on to them. Years after my return to Scotland, I still had many contacts in Africa. One of my Kenyan friends, Mrs. Eraj, a doctor's wife, asked me to select a house in Glasgow for her to buy. I duly bought a nice flat for her at Charing Cross, and she began to send me the money for the property in instalments. Meanwhile I found suitable tenants to occupy the flat and I accounted for the rent to my friend in Kenya.

Being a well-organised lady, Mrs. Eraj altered her Will to include the Glasgow flat. In the Will she stated: *"I have no debts. But I do have a small account with Mrs. Anne Good who collects the rent of my flat. I may owe her a few pounds, she might be having a few pounds of mine. Her words as to the state of our account will be absolutely correct, she is just about the most honest and honourable person I know."*

I was very touched by this description, which is as much a tribute to my parents as it is to me, because I learnt my morals at their knee. They were the only people I ever knew who were as honest as my husband, Rankine Good.

INDIAN CONNECTIONS

Working at the Lady Grigg Indian Maternity Hospital in Nairobi I naturally got to know many Kenyans whose families had emigrated from India. However, my closest ties were with the family of Jaswant Singh, and we remained firm friends after I had returned to Scotland, and the Singhs had left Nairobi for London. They later went home to India. My god-daughter Mira grew up into a handsome girl who read Law just as her father had done. But instead of going on to practise as a solicitor, she got married in 1979 to an Indian businessman, Ranjit Singh. I was delighted to be invited to the wedding in Dehli.

Afterwards the celebrations continued in the northern town of Jalunder, where Ranjit's father, General Bupinder Singh, was stationed. We were not far from the greatest Sikh shrine, the Golden Temple of Amritsar, and so General Singh organised a visit there. The building itself was an amazing sight, but I was embarrassed to see it surrounded by Western deadbeats. Because pilgrims travel to Amritsar from all over the world, the better-off Sikhs pay for meals to be served to all comers. Among the pilgrims I saw a crowd of besandled and be-spectacled white lads who looked like students, sponging off the free food. 1979 was part of the hippy era when hordes of Westerners travelled to India and Nepal for 'enlightenment' – or was it illegal drugs? In that part of India both opium poppies and marijuana grow like weeds, and anyone who wanted a cheap high could get it there.

It was some three years later, in 1982, that I returned to Dehli for the wedding of Mira's brother Sitender. This was a very happy occasion for us all. I took the opportunity of trying to help a fellow Lewisman. Perhaps some of my older readers will remember the sad story of the two female British students who went on holiday to Kashmir; one of the girls – as I call them in my old fashioned way – was Alison MacDonald, from Stornoway. She disappeared and was never traced, despite desperate efforts by her father and other relatives. There was no suggestion that these two students were into drugs or anything else disreputable. Alison was a Christian and her companion was a hard-working medical student. Some people speculated that Alison might have fallen into one of the mountain rivers and been drowned. Others feared that this attractive young girl had been seized by some of the many soldiers stationed in the area who had then killed her. Her father clung to the theory that she had been kidnapped by an Indian admirer and she was well-looked after, though unable to leave his house.

While I was in India for Sitender's wedding, I made enquiries about Western girls living with Indians. I got a tip off that a white woman called Alison, who was about the right age, was living in Jaipur, a northern town not far from Dehli. Jaipur is, of course, a long way from Kashmir, but it was quite feasible that if

Alison was being held in a harem she could have been taken there. My sister Zena had accompanied me to the wedding, and she now came with me by bus to Jaipur. At the bus station we were mobbed by taxi cyclists eager to get us into their vehicles. We didn't let ourselves be intimidated, but stuck to our plan to search for Alison MacDonald. We made enquiries at many shops and offices but drew a blank. Later Mr. MacDonald went to Jaipur himself and learnt that there was not just one Westerner called Alison, but several living locally. Sadly none of them was his missing daughter, just girls who had fallen in love and decided to make their homes in India.

Alison MacDonald's father returned repeatedly to the village where she had been seen last, and his search ended only with his death some twenty or so years after his daughter had vanished.

It was in the mid-1980s that I got to know another Indian, Dr. Prasad. He was already a qualified doctor of medicine when he came to lodge with me, but he had to pass additional examinations before he could fulfil his ambition to go to work in the United States, where one of his uncles was a prominent pathologist. He quickly qualified to work in the UK, but talented though he was, he had no luck with the US Exams. Prasad found himself staying in Scotland longer than he had planned. Of course he had no difficulty in finding work; I used to drive him to and from his post at Glasgow's Stobhill Hospital, because he worked such long hours on that isolated site. The poor man had even less time to himself than I had had as a trainee nurse in the 1940s.

The American uncle very kindly invited my sister Zena and me to join Prasad on a visit to the family home in Bangalore. During our stay, I was very anxious to visit the famous Hindu holy man, known as 'Baba' (Father) who lived some two hundred miles away from my hosts' home. To my surprise, Prasad's family thought this was a terrible idea. I am not sure if they disapproved of Baba because they were scientifically-trained doctors and he was a faith healer, or whether they had some hint of the scandal that was to erupt later. The reason they gave was that I would have to sleep on the floor at his compound. "Better people than I have slept on the floor," I retorted. I stubbornly set out to see the guru, travelling all the way by public bus, only to discover he was away.

It was not until a year or two later, when I interrupted a holiday in Kerala (South India) to visit Bangalore again, that I had an audience with Baba. Prasad's family seemed touched that I had made the effort to travel all the way from Kerala by bus to visit them, and they took me to see the guru. Also, something had happened in their own circle to change their attitude to Baba. One of Prasad's sisters-in-law had suffered from a serious respiratory infection which would not go away. With all their medical connections, the family could and did get the best orthodox treatment for her, but nothing would relieve her. Then she was taken to Baba, and her symptoms disappeared very quickly!

I was impressed by my visit to Baba's compound. We arrived early in the morning and stayed all day. The guru walked through the crowd of hundreds who had come to see him. People held out letters asking for his help. He would speak to certain people – apparently at random – and accept some but not all of the letters. He did not take the letter I offered him at the audience.

At the end of our holiday, Zena and I had several hours to wait at Mumbai (Bombay) Airport. She is a reader, but I prefer to pass the time writing. I decided to write to Baba, telling him that the Schizophrenia Association of Great Britain was short of £20,000 for a research project. I posted the letter before I flew home from India, and on my arrival I reported to Mrs. Hemmings, Director of SAGB. Within one week of my return, Mrs. Hemmings telephoned to say that the sum we needed had been offered to the Association in the name of a young Indian, Balwant, who had suffered from schizophrenia. The poor young man's estate was almost wound up, when a newspaper article on SAGB caught the lawyer's eye and he offered the £20,000 to the Association. Call it one of Baba's miracles, or just a coincidence, but I was very grateful.

Recently Baba has been accused of taking advantage of his position to interfere with young disciples who though not children were certainly below the age of consent. Dozens of pages on the internet are devoted to accounts of the scandal, but from several thousand miles away in Scotland I cannot tell you what the truth of the matter is. Whether the guru has indeed abused the trust of his followers, or whether jealous people have maliciously slandered him, it is a sad, sad story.

It was some three years ago, in 1999, that I paid my last visit to India. Once again I was with friends. During a visit to the USA I had got to know Dr. Barua, and his Christian wife, who was also a doctor. "Come to Calcutta," they said, and so I did. I stayed with Dr. Barua's brother-in-law, Dr. Telukdar, an eye specialist, in his big house outside Calcutta near the Ganges. I was treated like a queen, with a chauffeur at my disposal! I was very grateful for this, because the roads were so busy that I do not think I could have managed to get about alone. As well as the normal traffic hazards there were dozens of holy cows on the roadway.

I was very interested in the house in Calcutta where Mother Theresa had lived and worked. As a Christian and a nurse I was fascinated by her story. Conventional medical wisdom is that when you have to decide which patients to treat first, you perform Triage. Suppressing your feelings you look at each patient objectively and decide who might survive given immediate treatment, who could stand waiting before being attended to, and who is beyond human aid. You

Agnes Bojaxhiu
Mother Theresa of the Missionaries of Charity

treat the first category, then the second, hardening your heart to the third. Yet Mother Theresa had devoted her life to caring for hopeless cases. She had picked up dying people from the streets of Calcutta and lugged them home on her back. If the local neds made her drop her burden, she just picked them up again and staggered on. She had made special efforts to collect abandoned children from the streets. There was no hope of saving most of them – she was content to give them some love and attention before they died, instead of leaving them for the stray dogs.

I would have loved to have had the opportunity of talking to Mother Theresa. Reading her biography, I see that her struggle to be accepted as a nun was a lot worse than the difficulties I experienced qualifying for nursing school and passing the exams. And once she had taken the veil, she experienced a lot of hostility to her 'irrational' decision to concentrate on care of the dying. It was over twenty years before she was allowed to give up teaching. Now that Mother Theresa is a by-word for devotion and self-sacrifice, it is surprising to read that the local archbishop told her to quit as a nun if she wanted to work outside the convent! It was only after she had appealed to the Pope that she was allowed to follow her vocation, caring for the poorest of the poor.

But I was too late to meet Mother Theresa, and I had to be make do with visiting the place where she had worked. I saw her very plain bedroom, and the shrine set up after her death where there are daily prayers.

Now that I am over eighty, I probably will not be visiting India again, but I am glad to say India comes to me in the shape of many visitors, telephone calls and now e-mails!

'Mother Theresa' Anne and Mrs Telukdar

ANIMALS

By the time I was born in 1919 very few Lewis folk actually shared their house with the farm animals – the old 'but & ben' arrangement – but the livestock, especially the sheep, played a big part in our lives. As a result, I have been daft on animals since I was a little girl. Every spring there would be orphaned lambs in our kitchen. Many of these wee darlings survived, and though sheep are supposed to be stupid animals, they never forgot the good times they had enjoyed inside the croft. One ewe I remember particularly would never go out of sight of our house. Other sheep might wander farther afield in search of grazing, but she always stayed where she could see the building, even when she was a mother herself.

Another of the orphan lambs grew up to be a big strapping ram. One day when he already had a good set of horns on his head, he came visiting us. Entering the kitchen, he got the scent of the bannock which Mother had just cooked, and bold as brass, he grabbed the hot cake off the griddle. Mother went to chase him, and as he fled, his curly horn caught the handle of my favourite 'John Barleycorn' mug. The ornament hung on his horn for a moment or two and then smashed on the floor.

There was usually at least one cat living with us, and often a dog too. Looking back, I think how lucky my sisters, brother and I were to have the experience of growing up surrounded by animals.

When I was working in Kampala, I soon became known as an animal lover, and so whenever anyone went off to Britain on leave, I would find myself looking after his dog! One big crossbreed took such a fancy to me that he didn't want to go back to his real owner. 'Satan' as the dog was called would keep on returning to my bungalow long after his man had come back to Uganda.

Though I like most animals, there was one incident during my time in Africa when I would happily have slaughtered a whole troop of monkeys. My sister Zina and I were enjoying a short holiday at the famous Treetops Hotel. Early in the morning I heard a noise, and I thought it was my sister making her way to the toilet. But when I got up later, I discovered that my teeth had disappeared from the box beside my bed – those early morning sounds must have been caused by a monkey reaching into the room! I got dressed and rushed out to find the member of staff who had warned us when we arrived about marauding monkeys. He organised a search along the side of the lake, but there was no sign of my teeth.

Luckily the African manager I had been chatting to the night before came to the rescue. He knew the monkeys' habits and he went straight to a crag at the side of the lake. He found my teeth abandoned on the top of the rock and he quickly returned them to me. I was so relieved to get them back, I popped them in my mouth right away. Over breakfast I learnt that most of the guests had lost something to the monkeys. Spectacles and other things left on bedside tables had been taken. One of the other women was amazed that I had taken the dentures back after a monkey had chewed them – but what would you have done – gone home to Britain toothless?

During my years in Africa I made several trips 'up country' and visits to game reserves – but I won't bore you by talking about sights which you can see on the Discovery Channel every day of the year. Enough to say that I enjoyed seeing God's beautiful creatures living in the wild.

The most upsetting thing about my departure from Kenya in 1966 was having to leave my darling great dane Honey behind. I could not afford to put her in quarantine in the UK for six months, and in any case I think it is cruel to cage a pet animal for such a long time. Honey was a big dog, but very gentle and affectionate. I arranged for her to go to a man in another part of Kenya who raised great danes for show, but she tried to jump out of the vehicle that was taking her to her new home. Perhaps I should have had the

Honey

courage to have Honey put down when I left the country, but I convinced myself that she would be happy with a new owner. I later learnt she had died within a few months. Strange as it may seem after more than thirty years I still think of that wonderful dog.

My Siamese cat, Rakhi, is the only animal in my Glasgow home, but I keep a big toy sheep as a reminder of all those petted lambs in the Orinsay kitchen.

2002

If you have travelled a lot and you live to a good age, you inevitably lose many friends and acquaintances. I am lucky that at the age of eighty-two

John Nicolson Annes Brother a veteran of the Royal Navy in WW II, still living on the family croft

Zena Nicolson and Arthur Pollock The Beginning of fifty happy years

I still have the company of my three sisters and my brother, as well as nephews and nieces. My aunt, Christina Campbell, who squeezed past the bales of tweed to visit Number 12 Havelock Lane, is enjoying life at the age of one hundred.

My brother, John Nicolson, still lives on the family croft, and works as hard as his poor sight will allow.

My sister Joan, had the terrible misfortune to lose first her husband and then two fine sons. However she has rallied herself, and is at present in Stornoway caring for our sister Cathy, who is unwell. Joan's surviving son is an accountant in Madras. Daughter Morag, is married to Ian Davidson, currently Labour MP for Glasgow Pollok. Joan's other daughter Joyce is studying for her BSc in Nursing while working full-time in a nursing home. Who knows, maybe one day she will become the Professor of Nursing that I had dreamt of being!

Yet another niece, Gillian Pollok, is gifted in an entirely different way. Since graduating in Marketing, she has enjoyed a successful career. She worked in France and Spain, helping to launch new shops, before moving to South America for a couple of years. Of all the many places she visited, the Catalan city of Barcelona is her favourite and she has bought a house there. Meanwhile her sister Catriona is a veterinary surgeon with a busy practice in London and an even busier social life. The third Pollok sister, Kirsty, is happily married with a family.

If you look at the externals of my nieces and nephews' lives, they are far, far removed from the world of Orinsay and the family croft. Yet if you look into things more deeply, you will see that they are exercising many of the same talents that my parents devoted to their family, their crops and their animals.

As I get older, I spend more and more time reminiscing about my childhood on Lewis, where I was lucky to have many good friends as well as a big family. Sophie Kennedy was my best friend when I was a girl, and we had some great laughs together, sneaking off to the road dancing to meet boys, and so on. I am glad to say she is still around, and we keep in touch. The only other survivor of Sophie's family is her brother Callum, who enjoyed such success as a Gaelic singer in the 1970s. He is retired now and lives in Banchory. Though Callum's wonderful voice has been damaged by illness, his musical talent has been passed down to his daughters, particularly to Fiona and Christine who are professional singers themselves.

My Orinsay friend, Ishbel MacMillan, still lives on Lewis, just a few miles from where we ran wild as children.

May Doran who had accompanied me to East Africa eventually married and settled in Australia to raise a family. May died some years ago. Her eldest son, one of my god-children, farms near Perth and I hear from him regularly. May's widower, Pat Butler, is a good friend of mine who visited me here in Glasgow recently.

John Gillon, the man who sponsored May and me when we applied for work in Uganda, always was the life and soul of the party. I am pleased to say he is still very lively at eighty-eight years of age.

I am still in touch with one of the Roman Catholic priests I met in Kenya in the 1960s, Fr. Sheridan, who now lives in Kimmage House, near Dublin. Another resident was the priest who had been so kind to the Kenyan prisoners on death row at Kamiti. When I went to visit I took him a bottle of whisky, but sadly he had become senile and he did not seem to know me. We couldn't swap stories about the old days in Nairobi. I gave him the whisky but he ran upstairs with the bottle – as if to plank it! I hope he was later able to enjoy a dram with the other retired priests.

My god-daughter Mira is still happily married to Ranjit. Their daughter, who was just a baby when I saw her in Lucknow, is now dux of her high school, and she is looking forward to a university career. One of my last overseas trips was to visit the family at their home in Chandigarh. They gave me a wonderful time, taking me round all the sights. My thoughts are with Mira at this time (summer 2002) because she lost her mother recently.

If at first you don't succeed, try, try, try again – I

Mira, Anne and Ranjit

am glad to report that Dr. Prasad and his wife were finally accepted as immigrants to the USA. Today he has a profitable private practice, which she manages very efficiently. Their two sons are doing well at school, though it is too early to say what career they will follow.

Meanwhile Dr. Markose, Rankine's former colleague, is still in Dorking waiting for his wife to retire (she is a civil engineer), so that they can both return to India and a leisurely life on his coconut plantation. However their only son, a radiologist, plans to remain in England.

Another medical man, Dr. Ian Menzies, who once travelled all the way from Dundee to Stornoway to speak on allergies, is enjoying his retirement in Scotland. He was the man who urged me to write a book – I hope he approves of the result.

I was on good terms with the servants I employed in Kenya, but we did not keep in touch. I hope they and their families have been spared the curse of Aids which is sweeping Africa.

My home in the West End of Glasgow is open to any Lewis folk who happen to be passing. Many people find it convenient to spend a night at my house in Glasgow before catching plane or train to other destinations. It is a pleasure for me to give them hospitality, because they always bring me news of home, what the grandchildren of my old school friends are up to. I have been told that there is an Internet website devoted to the Orinsay area, but I am old-fashioned enough to prefer to hear the gossip in Gaelic. English speakers are welcome here too and I have an Indian lad staying in the spare room. I like to keep open house; if all the beds are taken, then guests are invited to sleep on the floor.

I no longer go round with a collecting tin, but my talent for fund-raising has not deserted me, as I discovered last summer. It was well after 11pm when I remembered that I would need cash early the next morning. All the local shops were shut, and so I decided to visit a public house to change the £20 pound note I had. My knee was hurting and I limped badly. What a pathetic sight! A little old woman, probably a hopeless drunk, hobbling along Woodlands Road at midnight . . . Just as I reached the Uisge Beathe pub a man who was heading the other way thrust something into my hand, and strode off without saying a word. I looked down and found that he had given me £1.25. The bar staff laughed their heads off when I told them. But wasn't it kind of the stranger to give me the price of a dram?

Since that mock election in the Lemreway School back in the 1920s, I have been a staunch Liberal, and today I am a member of the Maryhill LibDem Association. Thanks to the LibDems, I have met many interesting people, including the present Minister for Justice, Jim Wallace, who is doing so much for the new Scottish Parliament.

I was raised in the Free Church of Scotland, but these days I am a member of the Church of Scotland. The folk at Gardner Street, Partick are very obliging, and someone usually gives me a lift home after the service. Special thanks to Malina and Angus K! I don't feel embarrassed about accepting, because when I was a car owner I did the same. The minister, Roderick Morrison, is a wonderful preacher, as we would all agree.

More than three decades after I attended that initial course in Meditation, I am a regular visitor to Diana Kraz's Centre in Clouston Street, Glasgow. Though I regularly meditate in my own home (with the 'phone unplugged, of course) I feel that I meditate better in a group, and over the years I have taken a number of courses to learn more about the subject. As well as courses in Transcendental Meditation (TM) the Clouston Street Centre offers consultations in Ayurdevic medicine.

I have tried to share the benefits of meditation with people I think need it, eg victims of severe depression, but the cost of the training has risen so sharply that this is no longer possible. In the 1970s I paid £20 for my first course – now an introduction to TM can cost as much as £500! Fortunately some training is available free of charge, for instance in prisons, where it can help the inmates cope with the stresses of being locked up, overcome addictions, manage their anger and so on.

Though I am no longer active in the Schizophrenia Association of Great Britain, I retain my interest in people unlucky enough to suffer from this condition. Though my own health is not brilliant, I can help some schizophrenia patients by giving them a bed for a few days while the people who usually care for them are away or busy with something like decorating the house. By testing my temporary guests for food allergies I can perhaps ease their symptoms. In spite of all the drugs that have been developed to treat schizophrenia, there are a lot of people whose lives are wrecked by the condition, and so every little helps. I also give hospitality to other ex-mental patients, such as manic depressives. It's a pity that I am no longer fit to go down to George Square at night to distribute food to homeless people there, but I do what I can from my home.

Shortly after my eighty-second birthday, I had the satisfaction of seeing my name included in *'Who's Who in Scotland'. The Stornoway Gazette* reported that I was listed, which made me even happier. The picture I chose to accompany the entry was – of course – one of me in nurse's uniform, because 'Sister Annie' is what I have been called ever since I was at Primary School in Lemreway.

Our Lord had a lot to say about Lost Sheep and shepherds looking for them. Back home in Orinsay, when one of our sheep went AWOL, father would ask: "Where was it she got the milk?" Because he knew that sheep always remember where they were fed as lambs, and like the ex-orphans which kept barging into our kitchen, they try to return there. Then like the Good Shepherd in the parable Father would head for the remote patch of moor where the sheep had been suckled, and more often than not he would find her grazing on her home turf.

Now that I am getting older I am thinking more of home, hoping perhaps to spend the last days of my life back home in Lewis and be laid to rest there. I have enjoyed my travels to Africa, India and the rest, but at the end of the day you will find me like the sheep that goes astray, found where she got the milk.

Tha mi coltach ris na caoraich a tha a' dol imrall - mar as trice thèid and lorg far an d'huair iad am bainne.

Make your way to Stornoway
On the road to Orinsay
Where my heart returns each day
My lovely Stornoway

Retired Orinsay nurse in 'Who's Who'

A retired nursing officer from South Lochs who has been involved in many charities over the years will feature in the latest edition of 'Who's Who in Scotland', *writes Donnie Macinnes.*

Eighty-two year old Anne Good (nee Nicolson) from Orinsay has had her name entered in the book which will be published in March.

"I was taken aback when they wrote to me telling me that I was to be included in the book. I phoned to say I was too old but they said that age had nothing to do with it," said Anne who now lives in Glasgow. "They do the researching themselves as to who should feature and I was told it was an honour to be entered in the book."

Since she returned from Kenya in 1966, Anne has been involved with many charities. She has been Director of Schizophrenia (Scotland), as well as being founder of 'Action Against Allergy' (Scot) and is a 'Certificated Dowser'. She tests sensitivity to foods for people, free of charge, from her own home.

Anne has also been involved with charities inolving the homeless for a long time.

'Who's Who in Scotland' will be on sale to the public, priced £40.